ROUTLEDGE LIBRARY EDITIONS:
POLITICAL THOUGHT AND
POLITICAL PHILOSOPHY

Volume 37

THE FORM OF IDEOLOGY

THE FORM OF IDEOLOGY
Investigations into the Sense of Ideological Reasoning with a View to Giving an Account of its Place in Political Life

Edited by
D. J. MANNING

LONDON AND NEW YORK

First published in 1980 by George Allen & Unwin Ltd.

This edition first published in 2020
by Routledge
2 Park Square, Milton Park, Abingdon, Oxon OX14 4RN

and by Routledge
52 Vanderbilt Avenue, New York, NY 10017

Routledge is an imprint of the Taylor & Francis Group, an informa business

© 1980 L. G. Graham, A. Grimes, D. J. Manning, D. H. Rashid, J. D. Rayner and T. J. Robinson

All rights reserved. No part of this book may be reprinted or reproduced or utilised in any form or by any electronic, mechanical, or other means, now known or hereafter invented, including photocopying and recording, or in any information storage or retrieval system, without permission in writing from the publishers.

Trademark notice: Product or corporate names may be trademarks or registered trademarks, and are used only for identification and explanation without intent to infringe.

British Library Cataloguing in Publication Data
A catalogue record for this book is available from the British Library

ISBN: 978-0-367-21961-1 (Set)
ISBN: 978-0-429-35434-2 (Set) (ebk)
ISBN: 978-0-367-22202-4 (Volume 37) (hbk)
ISBN: 978-0-367-22205-5 (Volume 37) (pbk)
ISBN: 978-0-429-27375-9 (Volume 37) (ebk)

Publisher's Note
The publisher has gone to great lengths to ensure the quality of this reprint but points out that some imperfections in the original copies may be apparent.

Disclaimer
The publisher has made every effort to trace copyright holders and would welcome correspondence from those they have been unable to trace.

The Form of Ideology

Investigations into the sense of ideological reasoning with a view to giving an account of its place in political life

Edited by
D. J. Manning

London
GEORGE ALLEN & UNWIN
Boston   Sydney

First published in 1980

This book is copyright under the Berne Convention. All rights are reserved. Apart from any fair dealing for the purpose of private study, research, criticism or review, as permitted under the Copyright Act, 1956, no part of this publication may be reproduced, stored in a retrieval system, or transmitted in any form or by any means, electronic, electrical, chemical, mechanical, optical, photocopying, recording or otherwise, without the prior permission of the copyright owner. Enquiries should be sent to the publishers at the undermentioned address:

GEORGE ALLEN & UNWIN LTD
40 Museum Street, London WC1A 1LU

© L. G. Graham, A. Grimes, D. J. Manning, D. H. Rashid, J. D. Rayner and T. J. Robinson, 1980

British Library Cataloguing in Publication Data

The form of ideology.
1. Ideology
I. Manning, David John
145   B823.3

ISBN 0-04-320138-5
ISBN 0-04-320139-3 Pbk

Typeset in 10 on 11 point Plantin by Trade Linotype Ltd., Birmingham.
Printed and bound in Great Britain by
William Clowes (Beccles) Limited, Beccles and London.

Contents

Acknowledgements	*page*	vi
Preface M. J. OAKESHOTT		vii
Introduction D. J. MANNING		1
1 Ideology and the Sociological Understanding L. G. GRAHAM		12
2 Ideology and Religion A. GRIMES		22
3 Ideology and Philosophy D. H. RASHID		38
4 Ideology and Theoretical Inquiry T. J. ROBINSON		53
5 The Place of Ideology in Political Life D. J. MANNING		71
6 The Uses of Ideological Language J. D. RAYNER		90
Postscript JOINT AUTHORSHIP		113
Bibliography		132
Index		134

Acknowledgements

The editor wishes to acknowledge the financial support given to the Durham MA course by the Social Science Research Council without which this book would not have been possible. He also thanks Mrs Dorothy Anson and Mrs Jean Richardson for typing the manuscript.

Preface

Some ten years ago a friend of mine, Dr David Manning, a lecturer in politics in the University of Durham, embarked upon an adventure: he designed a year's course of study for graduate students in politics. It had some conventional features, but its central concern was to be an inquiry. And anyone who succeeds in engaging graduate students in an inquiry is, I think, doing something worthwhile. The inquiry here was to distinguish and characterise a certain aspect of political activity, namely, beliefs which, without specifiying a programme of political action, express a political commitment and may be recognised as reasons for acting. Nowadays, such beliefs are often called 'ideological', and consequently the inquiry to be embarked upon was identified as the investigation of the form, or perhaps the meaning, of ideological discourse. Students in the politics departments of universities are often invited to study current allegedly ideological doctrines (liberalism or socialism, for example) and are perhaps urged to consider the merits and defects of their constituent beliefs, but without even troubling their heads about what sort of beliefs they are, and without considering 'ideology' as a distinguishable mode of thought and argument. But here what was to be considered was just this, the logic of ideological discourse.

It was a severe undertaking. But, almost from the beginning, the seminar in which it was pursued attracted some remarkably able students who not only readily took to what was afoot but became adept explorers on their own account. And among its (usually) eight or ten members there was, in some years, a particularly distinguished student who, later embarking upon a research degree in Durham, remained behind to help to initiate newcomers. Thus, the seminar enjoyed an unusual intellectual continuity.

My connection with it, and the reason why I am writing this preface, is that, from the beginning I was appointed the external examiner of the work the members of the seminar submitted each year for the master's degree awarded by the University of Durham – answers to examination questions and a dissertation. I held this office for ten years. It entailed visiting Durham each autumn to discuss the work of those who were passing out (to use a military expression) and to meet and converse with the newcomers. I knew them all by name and nature, and I had the opportunity of observing, over the years, the gradual formulation of some findings about the character of ideological discourse.

To follow a well-trodden path, to begin with the word 'ideology'

viii *Preface*

and to ask how it had been used, was found to confront the inquiry with an anarchy of linguistic differences which promised no prospect of illumination. Indeed, the only conclusion to be drawn from the classical use of the term was that it is, or has become, a worthless concept. A starting place had to be found elsewhere. The focus of attention was to be politics; that is, practical activity concerned with the institutions and arrangements of an association of human beings. And it was plausibly assumed that ideological discourse (whatever else it might be) was a specific form of discourse related to that engagement. And further, it was assumed to be a form of discourse, not concerned with making proposals for political action, but having to do with general beliefs which might relevantly be invoked in justification of such proposals. Thus, the task was identified as that of distinguishing among the various forms of discourse concerned with or used in political activity one which answered to this general description, and then to specify its character as exactly as may be and to understand not only that it is different from (for example) philosophical, scientific, technological, moral, or historical discourse but why this must be so and why these cannot take its place. The consideration that it might turn out to be an ideal form of discourse, no more than a coherent possibility, and not to be found uncorrupted or unqualified in any piece of writing, was not to be dismissed. And the appropriateness of calling this mode of discourse, when it had been specified, 'ideological' had to be considered. But these were matters of no theoretical significance.

This, then, was the task. And this book is a performance of the task. Its contributors have all, at one time or another, been student members of the Durham seminar. They are joined in a single enterprise, but each has undertaken to explore in his own way the aspect of the matter which most interested him. And the reader who does not expect a definitive doctrine but some modest enlightenment will not be disappointed.

M. J. OAKESHOTT

Introduction

The chapters of this book have different authors and it might be considered a collection of essays. But in so far as it is a single inquiry by persons whose approach to the subject has been formed in the context of one seminar, the reader may expect to find in it the continuity that rightly suggests that it is a co-ordinated work, if not an absolutely exhaustive and complete one. The postgraduate seminar on ideology in the University of Durham has run for a decade and the following study reflects its findings. Its main concern has been to generate a theory of ideology in the belief that no reasonable account of the nature of ideological thought yet exists in print. The first three chapters explore the grounds of the methodological break the seminar has made with previous investigations. They offer a critique of some current misconceptions of the form of ideological argument suggesting that conceptual confusion has led to a failure to solve the puzzles ideological talk presents to the student of political theory. The remaining three chapters mark out the limits of the intelligibility of ideology in the context of political thought and life following the direction indicated by the previous three. To locate the occasion for an adventure of this kind this introduction is devoted to outlining, and exposing the incoherence in, the classical account of ideological understanding developed by de Tracy, Marx and Mannheim. The variety of contemporary considerations of the form and significance of ideology precludes, in the body of this work, consideration of the contribution to the misunderstandings of the phenomenon made by these writers.

In the classical account the term ideology refers to the systematic exposition of what purports to be theoretical knowledge claimed by its advocates to be indispensable to rational conduct in social, economic and political life. In the case of those who have no confidence in the power of such a theory to afford guidance in the 'rational' organisation of human affairs the term is also used to imply that it is to be taken as an inappropriate, if not a spurious, representation of man's nature and circumstances. The distinctive feature of the classical application of the term ideology is that it performs both the function of identification and that of evaluation of a type of belief.

In its classical sense the term ideology was first used by the French

2 The Form of Ideology

materialist Destutt de Tracy at the end of the eighteenth century to refer to the study he characterised as the science of ideas: namely, the study of the origin of our ideas about the world in sense experience. He claimed this science to be the fruit of the attacks on scholasticism and metaphysics led by Bacon, Locke, Helvetius and Condiallac, and he judged that the maturation of the discipline could not have been more timely. The French Revolution had removed those in positions of authority who would suppress an inquiry designed to destroy the appeal of doctrines obscuring the injustice of archaic privilege. De Tracy attributed to ideology the power to demonstrate the relationship between experience and ideas, and the relationship between truth and a well-ordered human world. The French nation could now expect to acquire the social, economic and political arrangements calculated to realise every man's potential for spiritual and material well-being. With this project in mind de Tracy, and his fellow ideologues, designed a programme of popular education to underpin the progressive achievements of post-revolution government in the way that the teachings of the Roman Catholic Church had, in their view, underpinned the repressive institutions of the *ancien régime*. Their enthusiasm, if not the cogency of their arguments, attracted the attention of Napoleon, who was flattered to find himself cast by the ideologues in the role of liberator. While he found their support a useful adjunct to his proposed reorganisation of French society he was prepared to be identified with their views, but once he was obliged to recognise that, in the balance of power, the influence of the Roman Catholic Church was the superior weight, he ceased to pay lip-service to the programme of the ideologues. It was then that he dismissed ideology, equating it with doctrinaire and utopian ideas.

Marx, whose use of the word ideology did most to secure the place it now occupies in our vocabulary, retained the derogatory overtone supplied by Napoleon half a century earlier, but derived the deprecation from his conclusion that ideology is a view of man and society naively supposed to be unrelated to the class relationships dictated by the prevailing mode of producing artefacts. In *The German Ideology* Marx and Engels tell us that:

> Morality, religion, metaphysics, all the rest of ideology . . . have no history, no development; but men, developing their material product and their material intercourse, alter, along with this their real existence, their thinking and the products of their thinking. Life is not determined by consciousness but consciousness by life.[1]

It is part of this account of human consciousness that gives us to understand that during any given epoch the dominant ideology is that of the ruling class, the class which owns the means of production:

The class has the means of material production at its disposal, has control at the same time over the means of mental production, so that in consequence the ideas of those who lack the means of mental production are, in general, subject to it.[2]

According to Marx and Engels an ideology is a systematic attempt to demonstrate the rationality of the existing distribution of wealth and the social utility of the order in which the wealthy hold positions of power. It is invariably an apology for institutionalised inequality. For example, the bourgeois ideology of liberalism, when capitalism has reached an advanced stage of development, will be found to obscure the reality of class war by attributing to economic necessity the payment of a minimum wage to members of the working class. It encourages the working man to believe that he has the chance to improve his material condition, through competing with his fellow workers, when it might otherwise be obvious that, in the long run, competition must impoverish them all. Ideology has always, in Marx's view, been inseparable from a class experience and interest at variance with the progressively more universal experience and interest of those who make the major contribution to the creation of wealth. Such a limited view of reality cannot indefinitely arrest, although it does retard, the development of the more encompassing and appropriate vision of experience of the increasingly politically conscious and numerically superior productive class. Ideologies, because they are essentially static understandings of changing circumstances, are all destined for the dustbin of history.

According to Marx, dialectical materialism can alone evade the charge of being ideological. It is unique in offering a dynamic understanding of the process of historical change, and a clear picture of those human relationships which preclude the possibility of instability. Dialectical materialism not only gives an account of how class society will be transformed into classless society, it specifies the relationships which constitute the two conditions. As a 'theoretical' foundation of communist practice in both pre- and post-revolutionary society it is incapable of being rendered redundant by changes resulting from the informed actions of its adherents. Marx tells us that the historical process, which renders ideas which have been instrumental in bringing about change in human relationships apologetic, is at an end when the communist revolution has taken place. Unlike feudal or capitalist society, communist society excludes the possibility of an ideologist attempting to justify positions of privilege having a productive function of decreasing humanitarian significance. When, as will inevitably come to pass, the ownership of the means of production is communal, and each contributes to the welfare of all according to his ability and takes for himself according to his need,

4 The Form of Ideology

there will exist no class distinctions and hence no possibility of ideological distortion.

Marx's charge is that ideology is a subjective form of understanding in two distinct respects. First, ideology prescribes a conception of the mechanics of social, economic and political change rendered obsolete by the changes that inevitably followed man's subjecting practice to its guidance when, at a past stage of economic development, it was temporarily an understanding offering an effective guide to action. Secondly, it cannot avoid advancing spurious justifications for the human suffering that attends the chaos that is the result of action based upon it when it has become a materially baseless or archaic view of experience. This claim that ideology may disguise the injustice of class distinctions, which are the consequence of man being alienated from his species-being, or true-self, is related to the further claim that, in a world of change, ideology must misrepresent reality. The sense in which ideology is morally reprehensible follows from the sense in which it is intellectually suspect. In contrast with ideology Marxism embodies both moral and scientific truth. It alone stands in the relationship to human experience which is congruous at every point in time, and for all time. Its relevance to practice is universal.

After Marx the most influential use of the term ideology is that of Mannheim. In some important respects it is similar to that of Marx. For example, Mannheim accepts that ideology is a practical view of reality comforting to those with a vested interest in the survival of the existing social order. It cannot serve as the basis of 'rational' action by the underprivileged. He is prepared to follow Marx in claiming that it is invariably conservative and never at any time a view of the world suitably radical in the style of what Mannheim calls utopian thought. However, at the same time that he is prepared to follow Marx in this direction he is not prepared to go along with Marx's claim that his doctrine offers an a-temporal understanding of the process of historical development capable of directing action calculated to abolish incoherence in human relationships of the kind that is manifest in the most advanced stage of class conflict. Mannheim claims that all ideas about human nature and the human world are intelligible only in the context of a given historical experience, those that project the aspirations of men who would create a new social order, for example, the ideas of nineteenth-century socialists, no less than those which defend an existing one, as did those of the classical liberals. He classifies Marxism as nineteenth-century utopian thought – a view of the world no less partial than the ideology of liberalism. Utopians like Marx may identify the incoherence of ideologies like liberalism, but this does not imply that they themselves offer a comprehensive view of reality. Mannheim denies the possibility. He does not question the status of Marxism as partial knowledge of a given historical situation, but he does question its claim to be an a-temporal understanding of the universal process of social change. From the standpoint of the sociology of knowledge, all 'knowledge is distorted and ideological when it fails to take account of the new realities applying to a situation, and when it attempts to conceal them by thinking of them in categories which are inappropriate'.[8] Mannheim conceives Marxism to be, in the modern world, just such a distortion of reality. It is rooted in a past experience in a way comparable to that of classical liberalism. However, although Mannheim would have us believe that he has encompassed Marxism within his own account of the relationship between ideas and reality, and hence shown that Marx's use of the term ideology has always been at least potentially ideological, it is not clear that his own account of ideology could be objective in the sense that it could be shown that it can, in principle, be said to be true or false. Mannheim's understanding of ideology is of the same kind as that of Marx in so far as the objectivity of the evaluation of the truth of ideology it offers depends upon the demonstrable coherence of his theory of knowledge. This account of the relationship between ideas and reality has to be shown to be independent of, and hence immune to, historical change before it can substantiate the claim that ideological and utopian ideas are relative and partial. It is conceivable that Mannheim's own theory of knowledge rules out this possibility. His conclusion would appear to be comparable to that of a man from an island who has affirmed that all its natives are liars. It destroys its own claim to objectivity. If all our ideas reflect a historical experience then those of Mannheim are not exempt.

In an attempt to rescue his thesis from the threat of self-negation Mannheim offers us the suggestion that classless intellectuals without an active political interest in the distribution of wealth and power and, hence, uncommitted to a formulated ideology or utopia can achieve an objective understanding of social reality. He is aware that his claims about the character of ideology and utopia can be taken seriously only if it can be shown that his theory of knowledge is an account of the relationship between ideas and activity of the kind that can distinguish a biased, or socially determined, view from an impartial, or independent, view of the world. However, to demonstrate that his defence of the sociology of knowledge has this power he has to establish that the methodology of the sociology is of a different order from that of the political activist concerned to devise a doctrine calculated to arrest or stimulate change. For example, if the intellectual is to demonstrate the objectivity of his views to the ideologist and utopian he has to be able to prove that he has transcended the subjectivity of their understanding. In short, if Mannheim is to show that the intellectual can illuminate the world of those who

6 The Form of Ideology

live in the shadow of limited experience he has to specify the procedures by which the intellectual has escaped this kind of darkness. It will not do to claim, as Mannheim does, that the superiority of the intellectual's sociological understanding of the world is revealed by its being, for intellectuals, a more comprehensive, or less partial, vision than that of the ideologist or utopian. Its appearing more comprehensive to the intellectual will not prevent the ideologist and utopian seeing it from their own limited standpoints and concluding that it is biased. As they are characterised by Mannheim, the intellectual and ideological or utopian views are distinguished only by the different points from which they are views. They are not views that can be said to be distinct in kind because it has not been shown that they have been formed in a different way. The only indication Mannheim gives as to how an objective view can be distinguished from a subjective view of experience is the suggestion that those who possess the former will be found to have no personal interest in a particular distribution of wealth and power when writing about the human world. We are told that they are able to construct a total view of political ideas seen in their historical-social situation, because they belong to no particular class or social group. However, this argument affords no defence against the proposition that the sociology of knowledge conceived as 'a constantly renewed attempt at synthesis of all existent perspectives aiming at a dynamic reconciliation'[4] is nothing more than a manifestation of the interest of intellectuals in integrated social circumstances conducive to their being able to pursue their work in peace secure in the knowledge that their academic status will not be challenged. The threat of self-negation which the sociology of knowledge thesis advances against itself is not dispelled by the introduction of the classless intellectual. If it can be defended it must be defended on other grounds. We will now proceed to see that no such defence is possible, and that a demonstration of its impossibility also serves to demonstrate the incoherence of the accounts of ideology given by de Tracy and Marx which are, as suggested, similar to that of Mannheim in important respects.

The classical use of the term ideology has three distinctive applications. Each of them refers to a different type of thought with at least a minimum power to distinguish ideology from other theories. De Tracy's use of the term refers only to one particular theory, Marx's use to all but one and Mannheim's to one of two types of a class of theories. At the same time, in each case, the term is used either to approve or condemn what is called ideology as the coherent or incoherent substantiation of claims about the world. The first use of the term, that of de Tracy, applies to the discoveries which lead to our being able to specify the technical recommendations essential to the pursuit of well-being. Ideology in this sense is a science like medicine. It is the master science of man and society. As the antidote of nonsense, ideology is the potent cure for all the consequences of irrational belief. De Tracy necessarily succeeds in recommending ideology, on account of its objectivity, as something of value, just as Marx and Mannheim necessarily succeed in condemning it by defining it as a partial and subjective account of human nature and relationships. According to Marx and Mannheim the adherent of an ideology cannot avoid revealing his bias when he acts in the world. It is manifest to the objective observer in the eventual futility of the ideologist's goals, and the diminishing efficacy of the means he has selected to pursue them. In all three cases the evaluative application of the term ideology is inseparable from its classificatory use. Neither de Tracy, Marx nor Mannheim uses the term to refer to a theory, or theories, that can be identified without reference to its, or their, having or lacking truth-value. It is this dependence that guarantees the evaluative power of the term. It follows that if we can demonstrate that the claims of de Tracy, Marx and Mannheim regarding ideology have themselves no truth-value, to object to their work as ideological in their sense, paradoxically, does express the kind of objective evaluation they believed they had achieved.

Let us examine the objection that can be brought against the claim that the use of the term by either de Tracy, Marx, or Mannheim is in accordance with a rule that guarantees the communication of an objective judgement. First of all, it is necessary to define the target of the attack.

It appears, on first comparing de Tracy's use of the term ideology with that of Marx, that there is no connection between them. De Tracy uses the term to refer to the science of determining the origin and application of ideas and Marx to the misrepresentation of the appropriate relationship between productive functions and consciousness at a given time. However, consideration of the two applications reveals that they are closely related. The grounds on which Marx advances the claim that ideological thought is subjective are grounds of the kind on which de Tracy based his claim that ideology is the objective study of experience; namely, that the proper study of the relationship between consciousness and the world falls within the discipline of science. Marx cannot, for example, condemn liberal ideas as subjective consciousness in the period immediately prior to the proletarian revolution without claiming that he possesses a theory that specifies what constitutes objective consciousness at this stage of historical development. A theory of this kind is in the order of what de Tracy called ideology. If de Tracy's claim that ideology is the objective science of ideas cannot be substantiated, the value he ascribed to the study is lost, and if Marx's claim that dialectical materialism demonstrates that ideology is subjective consciousness is mere assertion, then the derogatory implications of his classification of liberalism as ideology are dissipated. In both cases ideology will be rendered an empty category, since the attempt to specify what can alone be placed within it has failed. The application of the term by de Tracy and Marx must then be seen to be arbitrary; it will have been shown to lack a rule governing its application. Instead of enabling us to express an informed judgement about a view of the world it will only enable us to express our approval or disapproval of it. This will certainly tell us something about what the person who expresses the preference believes, but it cannot tell us anything about the status of his beliefs.

The same observation can be made on Mannheim's use of the term ideology once it is shown that what he calls the 'sociology of knowledge' is as dubious an intellectual construct as de Tracy's 'ideology' and Marx's 'dialectical materialism'. However, before we proceed with this demonstration it is useful to note an ambiguity in the claims made by all three.

De Tracy's claim is that the relationship between the world and our ideas about it is causal, but he also expresses the view that many of his contemporaries have false ideas about the world. The latter is incompatible with the former. Even if only true ideas are the product of sensation no man can be misled by Catholic priests. There is nothing experiential in what they say. The criterion of plausibility is rationality and this can have no place in the demonstration of a relationship in terms of cause and effect. Something like the same confusion occurs in the work of Marx. We are told that productive relationships determine consciousness and, at the same time, that certain ideas play a decisive part in determining productive relationships. We are told that it is the experience of their material existence that forms the ideas of the owners of the means of production, but that it is the ideas of the owners of the means of production that the employed accept, regardless of their own experience of material existence. Similarly, we are told that dialectical materialism demonstrates that certain ideas about the world will play a decisive part in shaping the course of events, because they accord with the present stage of history, when to have this power they have to be more relevant to the world in which men act, and the criterion of relevance is rationality not causation. Ideas that are the effect of experience are neither relevant nor irrelevant. They are necessarily what they are and nothing more.

Mannheim seems to be more aware than either de Tracy or Marx of the incoherence of an account of the relationship between ideas and experience which attempts the joint application of the concepts of causation and rationality. As we have seen his thesis is that our ideas about human relationships and practices are rational to the extent that they facilitate our participation in and control of them. Failure to adapt our ideas to accommodate the changed circumstances in which we conduct our lives must lead to increasingly ineffectual and frustrating social interaction. When this has occurred we may expect those people whose ideas are more coherent than the chaotic activities in which the ideological adherent is hopelessly enmeshed to change the world in accordance with their vision. We are given to suppose that the rationality of a practice, manifest in the relationships appropriate to its pursuit, sustains its existence, not that its existence causes us to hold the beliefs which make our participation in it possible. However, Mannheim has led us to believe that those who subscribe to an ideology stick to progressively more impractical ideas, because their vision of the world is partial, and its being partial is the effect of the fact that their experience of the world is limited. Ideologists move only in circles, and engage in activities, peculiar to their class – a class doomed to extinction. It is this limitation that prevents them seeing the superior coherence of the ideas of those more in tune with the times – those whose activity is increasingly the prevalent mode of existence. This, of course, is a determinist thesis, and one incompatible with the claim that the utopian can change the world, because his is a more coherent view of its potential. The ideas of the utopian cannot, in the determinist thesis, be seen to pre-date the experience they are said to create in the rationality thesis. They cannot, as the effect of experience, be the formative influence on practice. If ideological views reflect a given experience, so must utopian ones. Ideological and utopian ideas both have to be either the product of experience or the formative influence on experience. It is inconsistent to claim that although they are comparable, one is the effect of experience and the other the rationale of its pursuit.

To rescue the work of de Tracy, Marx and Mannheim from the charge of incoherence, those who claim to find it illuminating will have to found its conclusions either on the claim that experience determines consciousness, or that experience is the creation of rational understanding. Neither can both perform the task of explaining why men believe what they do in terms of cause and effect, and persuade them that holding one view is more rational than holding another. However, whatever can be salvaged by pursuing either of the two alternatives is destroyed by a further objection. Both theses are subject to a decisive refutation.

Let us first examine the determinist thesis. This can only prove plausible if it can be shown that we can distinguish between the cause, that which determines what we believe, and the effect, that which we believe, and this cannot be done in the case of experience of activity and relationships, and our beliefs about activity and relationships. It is the holding of beliefs about activities and relationships that makes the experience of them a logical possibility. Human activities and relationships have no independent existence in the world of the kind that constitutes the sensible in experience. There is nothing that we can locate with any of our senses that constitutes the world of programmes and activities, and the world of moral and legal ties. These are a manifestation of human identity and intelligence in the world, not a part of the natural world. Human activities and relationships are not phenomena that can be observed to occur in the way that, given a moving billiard ball strikes a stationary one, the moving one will have the effect of setting the stationary one in motion. It makes no sense to claim that our being familiar with practices and relationships X will cause us to hold belief Y. The experience of the conditions X is not, in this case, an event temporally prior to our believing Y.

We can now see that the incoherence of the causal thesis encompasses the incoherence of the rationality thesis. The holding of beliefs Y cannot precede the business of judging the world in accordance with what they prescribe. Adhering to a belief in what is of value in life entails evaluation according to it. A man who does not judge the world according to the beliefs of this kind he claims to hold is a hypocrite. We can, of course, have a premeditated plan to reform our practice and relationships, but our appreciation of its value depends upon the very same judgement that implies that our existing practice and relationships are unsatisfactory. No utopian vision, any more than an ideological one, in Mannheim's sense of the terms, can exercise an independent influence on practice. It is an integral part of practice. It constitutes the possibility of its intelligibility.

The human world is conserved, or reformed, by action, not physical change or ideas. Both the causal thesis and the rationality thesis about the relationship between ideas, on the one hand, and activity and the social order, on the other, require that the two be temporally discrete, when the relationship between them is necessarily a-temporal. It is a logical relationship. The existence of the one presupposes the existence of the other. The relationship involved finds expression in the understanding of a practice demonstrated by its appropriate selection and successful pursuit. Unlike the relationship between events in the physical world we call cause and effect, and the relationship between events in the human world we call action and result, the relationship between ideas and activity cannot be the subject of a narrative account.

It goes without saying that there is nothing remarkably sophisticated about the foregoing objections to what has been called the classical use of the term ideology. The appeal of the classical account of ideology taken out of its own ideological context originates in its charming simplicity, not in its intellectual achievement. And anyway, quite apart from the demands it makes on our credulity, the use of the term ideology by de Tracy, Marx and Mannheim, in so far as it is intended to persuade us to accept or reject particular ideological commitments, could not serve as a corner-stone in any well-constructed account of what is to be *understood* by ideological commitment in political life. That to which we may choose to adhere cannot serve in an account of adherence. Nevertheless, it cannot be denied that within the contemporary sociological account of the nature of ideological belief we can detect ideas inspired by Marx and Mannheim and that these marginally exceed in sophistication the form in which they made their original appearance. It has therefore been judged appropriate that the first chapter of this volume should demonstrate the irrelevance of the contemporary sociological approach to explaining the sense of ideological talk independently of the foregoing remarks, and on the level required successfully to conduct the rest of this investigation.

NOTES: INTRODUCTION

1 K. Marx and F. Engels, *The German Ideology* (Lawrence & Wishart, London, 1965), p. 38.
2 K. Marx and F. Engels, *Gesamtansgabe*, quoted in T. B. Bottomore and M. Rubel (eds), *Karl Marx, Selected Writings in Sociology and Social Philosophy* (Watts, London, 1956), p. 78.
3 K. Mannheim, *Ideology and Utopia* (Routledge & Kegan Paul, London, 1936), p. 86.
4 ibid., p. 152.

I
Ideology and the Sociological Understanding

Marx's aphorism that 'social being determines consciousness' is often referred to in the explanation of certain beliefs and practices by those with a sociological turn of mind. I have never been sure of the precise mechanism by which this determination is effected and I have never discovered any satisfactory account of it.[1] Indeed I am uncertain that any such account could be given. Nevertheless, the aphorism is closely connected with what I shall call the sociological notion of ideology. This rather vague and indefinite concept has, despite its vagueness, two concrete features which I propose to investigate. First, to describe a belief as ideological on this understanding is to fail to take it at face value, to point to something beyond the mere meaning and substance of the belief; and secondly, to call it ideological is to go some way towards explaining its currency by connecting it with the material interests of a social class.

I should say at the outset that what follows is not a critique of Marx or of sociology. In the first case what Marx had to say about ideology is so fragmentary that to reject it cannot be taken as a rejection of his whole system of ideas. In the second case, sociology is not confined to the explanation of beliefs in the manner I shall explore and quite possibly, for my knowledge on this point is scanty, such explanations are not even characteristic of sociological investigation as it is commonly conducted. But it is not to be supposed, on this admission, that the argument is set against straw men. It may be that there is no one school or particular kind of inquiry which has made the sociological notion its own, but recent writers on the subject furnish sufficient examples of this line of thought to make its examination worthwhile. Chief among these, perhaps, is Mannheim who states as one of his conclusions that 'each ideology, though claiming absolute validity, has been shown to be related to a particular position and to be adequate only to that one'.[2] More recently, Nigel Harris in *Beliefs in Society* supposes from the outset that

Ideologies do not exist, only people who have ideas, or groups which share ideas, many of which can have no significance at all for an isolated individual, only for someone who can presuppose membership of a group . . . Inevitably, ideas treated in isolation seem to be ritual, only accidentally related to what men do. Thus, explanations have to be offered suggesting that ideas are decorative features of an on-going process, or concealments of *real* drives.[3]

He concludes, among other things, that 'ideological analysis cannot fail in some measure to debunk, to devalue, the validity of all judgements, much as popular psychoanalysis debunks what we feel'.[4]

Another example is to be found in the writings of Professor Gellner who, though he does not use the term ideology very much, puts the sociological notion which I propose to examine to considerable use. This is especially clear in his discussion of the north African Berbers in which, with reference to the concepts of *igurramen* and *baraka*, he claims that 'here there is a crucial divergence between concept and reality, a divergence which moreover is quite essential for the working of the social system'.[5] And in general he seems to hold that the importance of social and political studies lies in their ability to uncover such divergences between belief and reality and the material causes of this intellectual distortion.

It should be evident, then, that though I shall not consider the exposition and modifications of particular writers in detail my argument will bear directly upon a good deal of influential thought upon the subject of ideology.

Consider the case of peasants who live in grinding poverty and are made to pay tribute of some kind to overlords whose affluence is evident. Of some of these peasants it may be true that the payment is made grudgingly and only, perhaps, because the overlords have means of enforcing payment at their disposal. There will be others, the majority possibly, who pay what they must neither grudgingly nor willingly but as a matter of course, accepting this as just another fact of their condition. But there may be some who claim that it is right and proper for them to make this payment, however hard it may be, and they may give reasons for thinking this in terms of a natural order, legal rights and duties, the concept of nobility, the idea of a creation ordained and sustained by God, or in some other way.

It will be plain that what I have outlined here is simply a sketch of the typical circumstances of ideological belief as it is understood by the sociological notion. In contrast to the first group, the second class of peasants consists of those whose consciousness of the *man-made* character of their condition has not been raised and the third is the class of those whose beliefs militate against their material interests and in favour of those of the overlords. If we convert the third class into a group of men and women who, though they offer abstract justifications for the payment of tribute, do not themselves make payment but are in fact directly or indirectly in the pay of the overlords, we have in the doctrines of this group a paradigm case of ideological belief after the sociological understanding.

Now the notion of ideology is intended both to pick out and to explain the essential differences between the last two groups and the first. That there are indeed differences to be described it is impossible to deny, though it is not obvious that having had them described already in terms of the beliefs and attitudes of the agents involved there is much more which needs to be said along these lines. It is less obvious still that there is anything peculiar about the existence or the conduct of these last two groups which calls for explanation. And if there is nothing abnormal or unintelligible in the situation I have described the provision of an explanation will be superfluous. This last assertion might be questioned of course, for someone might claim that it is as appropriate to explain the normal as the abnormal. I do not need to deny this. I claim only that to set out to explain the behaviour of the last two groups in the example is to suppose that their behaviour is odd in a way that that of the first group is not. But if there is something abnormal which requires explanation, we must ask what it could be.

One possibility might be this. It might be said that the fact that men gladly act contrary to their own material interests calls for some explanation. If a man truly understands that what he now does is to his detriment and to the benefit of another and that his own need is much greater than his beneficiary's there is something irrational about his acting in this way. But this is surely false. Actions of this sort are neither uncommon nor abnormal. The ordinary institution of promising, even between persons of the same social class, often gives rise to occasions on which it is right and reasonable for the poor to give to the wealthy, and in general the payment of debts and the observation of contracts is rational without any consideration of the relative prosperity of the contracted parties. Unless, then, we are to press the claim that all these actions are, in our common experience, irrational (a claim so audacious as to be absurd), we must admit that the actions of the third class of peasant in our example are not irrational *in themselves*, i.e. because of the kind of action they are, and are not, therefore in need of some special explanation.

Someone might argue that it is the explanations and justifications which the agents offer for their actions which make the actions irrational. For example, there is nothing irrational about a man's constructing a ship until he tells us that it is being constructed for use in an imminent worldwide flood, of which there are no signs whatever. Similarly, it is not the act of paying tribute itself which is irrational but this act in the light of the reasons for which it is performed, or at least, for which it is said to be performed. Plainly, this is a more promising line of argument, but not without difficulties. Whether or not a man's actions are irrational as a consequence of the beliefs for which they are performed depends entirely upon the content of those beliefs. Now the concept of ideology which we are investigating groups together the reasons of agents according to a common type rather than a common content. Thus beliefs about God, the moral law, the human condition and the state may all be ideological though their subject matter varies widely. The question arises, then, as to whether such a grouping is legitimate. This turns upon the characteristic by which they have been grouped. What this characteristic is differs from theorist to theorist. Let us consider first what I shall call the theory of unreal goals.

It is sometimes said that ideologies reconcile the agent to detrimental acts and conditions by presenting them as being ultimately to his benefit. There are at least two ways in which this may be done. First, in a conservative vein, the ideologist may argue that though certain acts are to the immediate detriment of the agent, the maintenance and survival of the whole social system depends upon their being performed. Consequently, though in the short term the payment of tribute to those who are more prosperous, or the acceptance of low wages to the benefit of the entrepreneur, is detrimental, in the long term both comprise the wisest course of action for the poorest labourer since without a social system he would have no means of subsistence at all. Alternatively, or in addition, in a religious vein, the ideological priest or theologian will argue that the harder a man's lot in this life the richer his reward in the next, provided he accepts his lot uncomplainingly. The ordinance of rights and duties emanates from a divine providence which ensures that all things work together for good and whose ways are as unquestionable as they are inscrutable. Now the theorist who claims that these doctrines are ideological may argue that such arguments and the beliefs they sustain make actions based upon them irrational for they are unreal goals. In the first case the conservatism rests upon the false assumption that there can be no other viable social system than that which presently exists, and in the second case, the irrationality arises from the postulation of an afterlife and a divine providence which is, variously, pure unverifiable fantasy, or psychological projection.

I do not want to become involved in arguments concerning what is here taken to be the truth of conservatism or the rationality of religion. It is sufficient for my purposes to note an important feature of the criticism of unreal goals which prevents it from being an elucidation of the sociological notion of ideology. The theory of unreal goals merely shows that the tribute-paying peasant has miscalculated. What he does would be perfectly rational if the goals he supposes to be real were real indeed. In both cases he imagines that in the long run he would be much worse off from not paying than from paying, but since, let us suppose, the destruction of the present system of social organisation would not render social existence and hence his own survival impossible, and since, let us suppose again, there is neither God nor immortality to ensure final retribution, he is simply wrong in what he imagines. But there is nothing special about his mistake which calls for an explanation in terms of ideology. In both instances the peasant's mistake is exactly like the mistake of the man who invests his life's savings in some South Sea Bubble, or of the man whose faulty arithmetic leads him to exchange an investment bringing a 14 per cent return before tax for one at 6·5 per cent where the tax is already paid. Such miscalculations are a part of everyday life and require no special explanation or classification. If all the talk of ideology amounts to no more than a new name for an old mistake there is nothing worth investigating in it.

Those who find the unreal goal theory attractive and are reluctant to accept this conclusion may urge that there is an important difference between the two kinds of case cited. In the case of the South Sea Bubble or the income tax advantage the false beliefs are easily arrived at and some considerable care is needed to distinguish them from true ones, while the doctrines of social conservatism and religious myth are manifestly false, and it is the acceptance of the manifestly false which requires explanation. But what, leaving aside the prejudice which begs the question, are we to take as the mark of the manifestly false? Even if we accept that such doctrines can be shown to be true or false it cannot be near universal agreement on what is to be taken as their falsity, for disagreement on what is said to be the truth of both these doctrines is widespread. Nor can it be absurdity. At worst the parallel is taken to be with a peasant who exchanges the coin he has in hand for the prospect of a pot of gold which some swindler assures him has been buried in the forest. The likelihood that there is such a treasure is contrary to our practical experience and expectation, but it is not inconceivable that gold should be buried in a forest. Nor can it be that these beliefs are manifestly absurd because they are accepted only by the ignorant and unthinking (as the suggestion that ideology is to be replaced by science seems to imply) for it cannot be denied that countless men and women of impressive learning and intelligence have subscribed to social conservatism and religious belief.

It seems, then, that the difference, if there is one, between ideology and simply mistaken beliefs cannot be brought out in terms of manifest falsity. Let us consider another possibility. Ideological beliefs, it may be said, are ideological in that they serve the interests of one particular class and are intended to be believed by members of other classes, while at the same time they are expressed in a form which disguises this advantageous relation to one class. So, for example, the doctrine that riches and poverty are unalterable facts of the natural condition of mankind, though it appears to apply equally to rich and poor, in fact serves the interest of the rich alone. It serves their interest by inclining people, the poor, who could disturb the economic system of distribution which makes the rich rich, to acquiesce in that system. The victim of ideology is a victim because his ignorance of the class interests served by the ideology to which he subscribes condemns him to irrationality, that is, prevents him from thinkingly pursuing his true interests, while the protagonist of the ideology, the ideologist, hides the fact which would expose the irrationality of accepting his doctrine.

Plainly the assumption which must be made by this account of the sociological notion of ideology is that the paradigm of rational action is the promotion and pursuit of effective means to material welfare and in its turn this presupposes that rational action is purposive in character, that reason serves action in the matter of calculating sufficient means to given ends. This Humean assumption may be defended in a great variety of ways and the task of showing the error in all such defences would be a very large one. But it is not necessary to do this. In order to show that this account of rational action is incomplete it is sufficient to point to the fact that it is our common practice to accept other, non-prudential, non-purposive sorts of consideration as proper occasions for practical thinking which may be rationally or irrationally conducted. Chief amongst these, perhaps, are moral considerations. As Kant has shown, I think, the man who urges some general moral principle and defends an action taken upon particular recommendations which make an exception in his own case is guilty of irrationality, not because what he does fails to promote his material interest or because there is no discernible purpose in what he does, but because his inconsistency is of a sort to make his advocacy of the general principle unintelligible.

Now if the purposive, prudential account of practical reason were as easily shown to be false as these brief remarks suggest, it would not have had the long history it has. The point I have made and the illustration I have given might be questioned in a number of ways. It may be said, for example, that the non-prudential considerations of which I have spoken are certainly influences upon conduct, but not rational ones. On this view it is moral emotions and feelings which prevent and promote certain actions. Again, of Kant's demonstration it might be said that the inconsistency which he claims to show has nothing in particular to do with action. It is none other than the inconsistency of believing 'whenever A then B' and believing 'A but not B', an inconsistency to be found at all levels and in any kind of thought. Both of these replies could themselves be answered, I think, and still further replies might be made to those answers but instead of pursuing this manner of argument I propose to short-circuit (so to speak) this lengthy if not interminable process by asking and offering an answer to the question: what do we mean by rational action?

When we call an action rational we mean first of all that it is an action which has a reason (or reasons) and further, since rational is a normative concept, that the reason is a fairly good one. To say that rational action is action with a reason, however, is not to say that the agent in question must have engaged in a preliminary piece of reasoning but only that reasons for acting in the way he has can be given either by the agent himself or by others, which reasons will serve to make his action an intelligible response to an understood situation. This is a point of the greatest importance for it enables us to see that the familiar contrast between reason and passion presents us with a false dichotomy. If it is the case that to attribute a reason to an action is *not* to say that it has been caused by a thought which preceded it, it is clear at once that feelings and emotions may themselves be reasons. For example. A man may resign his post in support of a friend and colleague he thinks has been unfairly dismissed. He may thereby sustain considerable loss in terms of earnings and prospects but we say that, given his affection for and feelings of loyalty towards his friends, his action is a rational one, whether or not we regard it as wise or sensible. It is rational because we can see an intelligible (and not merely a causal) connection between the treatment of his friend, his affection and his action, a connection given by the conception of friendship which the man shares with us. It is the possession of such a conception which can make the treatment of friends and colleagues an occasion for thought of the kind which has a bearing upon conduct, though not of the kind which calculates means to ends, even when such treatment has no effect upon our material interests or the desires which we have set ourselves to pursue. The question 'what am I to do?' when it is asked on an occasion like this is not the question 'by what means may I achieve my purposes and desires?' but 'what does friendship require of me?' To this question more or less good answers may be given but in any event they are to be arrived at only by thinking about the conventions of friendship. It is this which leads us to the possibility of calling such deliberations rational or irrational.

Similarly, the peasant who is faced with the demand for tribute has more than one manner in which he may think about it. In

Ideology and the Sociological Understanding

addition to the obvious considerations of material benefit and detriment the payment may be considered in the light of his conception of feudal rights and obligations, or in the light of his knowledge of God whose service, however arduous, is perfect freedom. It follows from this that even if the peasant fails to pay attention to the prudential aspects of this position altogether, it is still possible for his conclusion to be rational or irrational. Even if we suppose, therefore, as the protagonist of the notion of ideology I am examining supposes, that ideological beliefs are expressed in a form which disguises the real material effect of widespread adherence to those beliefs, we cannot conclude that the possibility of rational deliberation is denied to those who adhere to them. Of course, this is not to suppose that the possibility of rationality is always open, but whether it is or not depends upon the sophistication and coherence of the conceptions which may be employed. The conception of God with which Christians operate may be a radically incoherent one, in which case their account of worship will be unintelligible and to that extent their participation in it irrational. But whether this is the case or not can only be settled by reference to particular beliefs or sets of beliefs and cannot be decided on the *a priori* ground that beliefs of this kind allow no scope for (or overlook or hide) considerations of material good and bad.

Lest the full force of the point I wish to make should be obscured in the welter of argument, it may be well to repeat it with as much precision as possible. The sociological notion of ideology rests upon the assumption that to identify the *kind* of belief which men hold may, in certain circumstances, amount to explaining why they hold them. This can only be the case, however, if we may reasonably suppose that were the beliefs not of this kind, they would not be held. So we are told that ideological beliefs are those which bear a certain relation to the material interests of those who advocate and subscribe to them, but which are and must be expressed in a misleading form. They must be so expressed because if the relations which they bear to material interests were known and recognised, they would cease to be held. Why is this? The answer I have been considering is that such knowledge and recognition would amount to a recognition of the irrationality of holding such beliefs and acting upon them. I have shown, I think, that this is false. Someone might suggest an alternative answer, namely, that ideological beliefs would cease to be held, not because public recognition of their true character would make subscription to them irrational but because, as a matter of fact, men do not often subscribe to beliefs and values which are contrary to their material interests and could be expected therefore to abandon them. To advocate such beliefs then, in a straightforward way would be to render them ineffectual. But we must reject this suggestion for the following reasons. First, it entails that those who advance ideological beliefs wish to promote certain material interests but hide the fact that this is the point and purpose of what they do. For this to be possible they must themselves be aware of the deception and intend to deceive. Thus the suggestion involves an empirical claim about the motives and intentions of all those writers and theorists who have expounded and defended beliefs which could be called ideological, one that is plainly false. In fact I do not know of anyone who has wanted to advance this audacious historical claim and in most versions, this empirical element is either unnoticed or trucked out with references to some occult psychological mechanism (self-deception or false-consciousness) which saves the claim at the cost of unfalsifiable vacuity. Secondly, the suggestion not only entails empirical claims about countless men and women but itself amounts to an empirical claim about characteristic human behaviour, which is not obviously true and for which we have been presented with no evidence. Even if the first objection did not apply then, we could not endorse this suggestion without a great deal of empirical investigation.

I have addressed myself to particular arguments and *ad hoc* emendations to particular suggestions as the exploration of the subject has demanded. It may be necessary, now, to set out the conclusions of the argument as I understand them.

First, once we admit that men may reasonably be moved to act or to subscribe to a belief by considerations other than material advantage, we must acknowledge that *prima facie* there is nothing odd about the attitude and belief of the third group of peasants in the example with which we began, who believed that it was right and proper to pay their feudal dues to their overlords regardless of their own poverty and the affluence of those to whom the money would go.

Secondly, to argue that there is nothing odd about their belief is not to argue that it is the right one to hold in such circumstances, but rather that there is nothing which calls for explanation here. The belief may require and occasion argument, in defence or criticism of it, but it does not need to be explained away in terms of something else. If there *is* anything to be explained it must be some unusual feature of this particular case (that, for example, the peasants continued to believe this in the face of arguments which they themselves acknowledged to tell conclusively against it); not something peculiar about cases like this. This means that investigation into and explanation of specific historical instances is required and no general explanatory classification will suffice.

Thirdly, if there is something which needs explanation in some particular cases this is because they deviate from a normal or common pattern which must be taken as given without explanation. In short, if there are cases of peasants whose attitude of willing acquiescence in their own burdensome condition requires some explanation there must be similar cases which call for none. The same point can be made another way. If there are occasions upon which it is reasonable to wonder, in the circumstances, whether those who advocate this or that belief or course of action mean or realise what they are saying, this presupposes a contrast with occasions on which what they say is to be taken at face value.

The conclusion of the argument, then, is that situations like the one I sketched either call for no explanation at all, or, if they do, call for an explanation different in kind from that which the sociological notion of ideology can offer, an explanation, moreover, of a sort which presupposes that the beliefs involved have the substance and meaning they appear to have. This conclusion does not render all talk of ideology worthless. In fact I think there is a perfectly good use to which the word may be put and which does not involve the mistaken assumptions I have been examining here. Nevertheless, the notion of ideology with which I have been concerned is so widely accepted that there is a danger that any use of the term will be understood in this way.

NOTES: CHAPTER 1

1 An exposition and defence of the general idea, though not, it seems to me, a successful one, is offered by W. G. Runciman in his essay 'False-consciousness', *Philosophy*, 1969.
2 K. Mannheim, *Ideology and Utopia* (Routledge & Kegan Paul, London, 1936), p. 130.
3 loc. cit., p. 29.
4 ibid., p. 219.
5 E. Gellner, 'Concepts and society', in Bryan Wilson (ed.), *Rationality* (Blackwell, Oxford, 1970), p. 44.

2
Ideology and Religion

We are haunted, if not by the ghosts of dead concepts, at least by the ghosts of what are said to be dead prejudices. Though it is now usual for sceptics to pay lip-service to the fact that it was logical positivism and not God that suffered from a terminal ailment, many still see the philosophy of religion as conceptual necrophilia. Given the decline of Christianity, in what is increasingly understood to be a secular and scientific age, the task of combating religion – that is, of freeing men from a superstitious or outmoded set of beliefs – has been largely put aside in the belief that they will pass away without any help from philosophical analysis. The wrath of sceptics has now fallen on ideology; the secular illusion of the secular society. As Hobbes saw the ghost of the Roman Empire in the Roman Catholic Church, there are those who see in Marxism, nationalism and fascism the ghost of Christian religion in secular guise. For them, religion and ideology are lumped together, in the sense that both are seen as false doctrines or inadequate guides to action to be contrasted with 'a voice that, with impartial logic flays them all'.[1] They agree with Professor Raphael that an ideology may be taken to be 'a prescriptive doctrine that is not supported by rational argument'.[2]

In contrast most of those called ideologists and those who claim to be religious have been concerned to keep their beliefs apart; not least because they see their convictions as rivals for allegiance. Christians have wanted to emphasise the gulf between the sacred and the secular – the City of God is not seen to be the earthly city with better sewage disposal. Marxists and liberals have wanted to contrast what they see as religion with what they take to be philosophy and science. There have been some attempts at a theoretical level to see how much common ground there is between religion and Marxism or liberalism (the best known case being the Christian–Marxist dialogue), but the majority of adherents on either side remain unconvinced as to the suitability of a merger. Of the small group of Christian–Marxists who see themselves as a bridge between both sides, it has been unkindly remarked that there is a limited use for a bridge that touches neither side of the river. For the most part,

Marxists, as Francis Barker put it in a recent issue of *New Blackfriars*,[3] believe that because Christianity is an ideology it will be incompatible at a theoretical level with Marxist 'science'. Compared with Marxist 'knowledge', Christianity offers groundless confidence for action in the world. Liberals often conclude that religion, with its emphasis on authority, be it that of the Bible or the Pope, is repellent to reason and to the 'autonomous man'.[4]

In this Chapter I shall critically examine what, broadly speaking, are the claims of those who recognise no formal distinctions between ideology and religion and those who categorically reject their conflation. It is of the utmost importance that they are not confused, and to help avoid this it is first of all necessary that we specify that to which the terms religion and ideology are to refer. For the purposes of this chapter by religion we are to understand Christianity, and by ideology the beliefs that reveal the identity of Marxists, liberals, nationalists and the like. No evaluation of the beliefs involved is implied by this classification.

The first claim, that ideology and religion are distinct, is sometimes expressed as follows: whilst ideology is about man, and the here and now, religion is about God and the hereafter. It is, however, clear that in religious thought God is not evacuated from his creation. The study of Old Testament prophets such as Amos, Micah and Isaiah,[5] and the Last Judgement as related by St Matthew,[6] should be enough to show that human actions and relationships are not to be understood as being independent of religious faith, but rather as the occasion or context for an expression of that faith. To say that the Christian attitude to life is 'otherworldly', or 'spiritual', is not to conjure up a mysterious parallel world in which the Christian may claim to partake, but to talk about the standards used in judging *this* world. The 'spiritual' is not, *pace* A. N. Whitehead, what is left over when material things are removed. Such a view would run the risk for the Christian of making God's commandments remote from his creation. Fortunately for them the prophets and evangelists make clear the kind of relationship that exists within the Judaeo–Christian tradition between the love of God and the love of the neighbour. The latter, as St John points out, is not an optional extra which is chosen apart from the former, but the principal way in which the former is shown. Furthermore, as Kierkegaard tells us, love of the neighbour is not like love for another person that could legitimately fade away or even cease. The neighbour is always present and the necessity of Christian love of him or her is permanent by virtue of the existence of the Creation. Although for the Christian the religious and the practical are distinct in experience, they are both ever-present in it. They are also both aspects of the public world on which it is possible to make objective judgements.

24 *The Form of Ideology*

The Covenants of both the Old and New Testament are made, not with an individual, but with a people. The events that befall an individual, such as the conversion of St Paul, or the misfortunes of Job, are only intelligible within the context of the religious community and tradition of which they form a part. The concept of religious community is not something incidental to religion, but the context in which *religious* notions of truth and falsity are understood. What I am trying to combat here is the tendency, inherent in the dichotomy between God and the world, to make the latter public, and the former private. To speak of prayer, or our relationship with God, as private is not to place it outside discussion, but to suggest that it does not invite secular government. Prayer is discussable in the context of the religious tradition to which it belongs. To claim otherwise is to skate close to the troubles encountered by Schleiermacher in making religious claims self-authenticating.[7]

Now, the failure of the first claim does not establish that religion and ideology are identical. My point, however, is that they can both be said to play a similar role in a person's life. That is to say, for some, as the Christian sees the Resurrection as saving humanity from the power of sin, if only man will accept the gift of God's grace, revealed in the life and person of Jesus, so the Marxist may see the proletarian revolution as freeing mankind from capitalist exploitation, when the proletariat of the world unites. And, to extend the parallel one stage further, as the kingdom of God inaugurates 'authentic' human relationships (in the sense that they are no longer necessarily corrupted by sin and death), so the proletarian revolution ends 'pre-history' and becomes the starting point (not the culmination) of 'authentic' human history (in the sense of making it possible that human relationships be for the first time, uncorrupted by exploitation).

Of course an ideologist may well agree with what has just been stated and still claim that ideology and religion are distinct. As I said earlier, the Marxist conceives that religion is 'ideological' in the sense of being both a false and a biased view of the world, but that Marxism is not ideological, because the form of its claims is comparable to those of science. Marxism, it is claimed, can not only be shown to be capable of distinguishing true from false propositions about the world, it can explain why people such as Christians hold to false ones. For Marxists Christianity is not simply a false doctrine, it is an example of 'false-consciousness' or wishful thinking.

It is interesting in this context to note the similarity in the arguments offered against religion by Marx, Feuerbach and Freud. Indeed, Marx's own atheism seems to have been derived largely from Feuerbach, who saw religion as the 'dream of the human mind' telling us (in a pejorative sense) about the believer and not about

God. This was the result of applying Feuerbach's transformative method to, for example, St John's claim that 'God is Love', revealing that this really means 'Love is God', and so on. Marx extended this to cover material relationships, making Hegel's 'Man is the master of his property' reveal 'Property is the master of man'. However, whether religion is seen as neurosis on a grand scale, or the symptom of mankind's alienated essence, it still needs to be shown that it is false and irrational. This the argument does not try to do; for it *assumes* that religion is false, and therefore to be in need of explanation as a phenomenon, in the same way that we look for an explanation of X's paranoia when we have *established* that his claim 'everyone is against me' is false. In short, it attempts to explain mistaken beliefs without showing us why they are mistaken.[8] Without such a previously established sceptical conclusion it is easy to see that this devaluation of religious belief loses its force in the argument. That is to say, if we wish to say that religious beliefs are nothing but neurotic hankerings after the security of a father figure, or the product of certain material conditions, then we are open to the rejoinder that our own anti-religious beliefs are nothing but childish rebellion against our human father, or the product of material conditions. Reductionism of this sort neatly undercuts itself, since religion and atheism do not come out as the irrational and the rational, but *equally* as products of the psyche or society.

This is not to deny that some religious people are neurotic, or that people may turn to religion out of a sense of personal inadequacy. I am merely claiming that it is illegitimate to move from this fact to the claim that religion itself is a neurosis or a crutch for emotional cripples. This simply does not follow. To reach such a conclusion requires that neurosis be contrasted successfully with *normal* behaviour. On the face of it, many religious believers are completely normal, and more important, the most direct way by which we can identify a religious neurotic is by contrasting his or her behaviour with that of a normal religious believer. This being so, the criteria we must use to designate X as a religious neurotic must be those of authentic religious behaviour, and it follows from this that such a judgement must *presuppose* religious criteria and cannot stand in judgement on them. Another difficulty is that for both Freud and Marx nothing whatsoever can count as a falsifying example. In their description, *whatever* religious believers do they still offer mere rationalisations for doing it. Now, as we have noted, it is usual for correctly calling a given reason a rationalisation to rely upon the existence of appropriate criteria, but there is an important feature of the notion of deception, namely, the possibility of the person who is deceived being able to recognise it, that casts doubt on the rationalisation thesis altogether in the work of Marx and Freud. Lear, for example, eventually sees Goneril and Regan in their true light. But this is not open to those who suffer from 'false-consciousness' or a neurosis; for Lear's recognition of what has gone before, though it changes his perspective on matters, is still intelligible within the one framework. What Lear believed *could* have been true, and it is only the tension that exists between what Lear believes Goneril and Regan to be, and their actions (which indicate the opposite), that brings us to say that he is deceived. These features are, however, absent from the situation in which the Marxist or Freudian wishes to call religion an illusion. Here the beliefs *cannot* be the right ones. Their class or childhood experience prevents their recognising this.

Another way of bringing out the error involved in thinking that we can explain religion away by giving an account of the genesis of religious belief is to consider a distinction we can make between reasons as grounds and reasons as motives. I may, for example, assert that the Battle of Hastings was fought in 1066. My grounds for asserting this consist of the relevant historical evidence that we have at our disposal. These are independent of my will and that of anyone else. On the other hand, I may refrain from correcting someone who claims otherwise, my motives being that of fear originating in my knowledge of his violent temper. This response is independent of the standard of truth involved in the first case, and leaves the truth-value of the statement untouched. The two cases are such that they cannot be reduced to each other. There is a logical gap between them. We can have reasons of either sort, but a ground cannot be a motive and vice versa. We have grounds for claims and motives for *actions*. Jealousy may be my motive for killing X, but it cannot be evidence for it; the detective's photographs may be his grounds for suspecting my guilt, but a knowledge of my motives is not. Thus the location of the motives of a religious believer could not affect the truth or falsity of his or her grounds for faith. It should also be added at this point that such arguments will be valid against any such accounts of ideology as well. That is, those theories that attempt to see them as forms of wish-fulfillment or the externalisation of internal disorders.[9]

The ideologist may still not be convinced by this. In particular the claim may be made that we are indeed looking for grounds, rather than attempting to locate motive, and that the truth of the ideologist's prescriptions is demonstrable by an appeal to history, science, or philosophy. Thus the certainty of academic disciplines (if there is indeed such a thing) is contrasted with the lack (and in some cases, Karl Barth for example, the positive disavowal) of any foundation for religion in this sense.[10] However it is not clear that religious faith is compatible with the kind of certainty we expect of science or philosophy. Given certainty, what, as Kierkegaard asked, becomes of the possibility of faith? We can admit that there is a distinction to be made between the natures of knowledge and of faith, but the distinction is not one between that which is rational and that which is irrational. It is a formal difference, not a difference that depends upon an evaluation.

Another claim made, amongst others, by Patrick Corbett[11] and Alasdair MacIntyre,[12] is that Christianity is itself an ideology. Corbett, for example, takes 'the Marxist', 'the Catholic' and 'the (American) Democrat' as his main examples of ideological belief (although he claims that there are hundreds, if not thousands of other examples, including Ghandism, nazism, the divine right of kings and myths about the English public school!). There are two points that can be made about this characterisation. The first is the systematic unfairness of it all. His account of Catholicism ranges at points between a parody and a travesty. He writes:

> His [the Catholic's] contempt for fact is so glaring as to need no comment. His fundamental contention is that the ills of the world . . . can only be cured by the acceptance of certain truths . . . under the guidance of the Church. Now if this were true there should plainly be some correlation between the power of the Church and the peacefulness of life . . . but as everyone knows, the truth is exactly the reverse.[13]

This 'must be seen by anyone who looks without prejudice at the world around him', though 'looking at the world without prejudice is not the Catholic's aim . . . he is prepared to spin the facts around in any way that suits his purpose'.[14] I cannot actually think of any Catholic theologian who believes that the ills of the world can be *cured* in the way that Corbett describes, nor anyone who thinks that the truth of Catholicism is shown or measured by the correlation Corbett suggests. It is, of course, the duty of the church to bring people to God, and to uphold certain Christian values, but even so the ills of humanity could not be cured by the church, since these ills are a condition of sin which must always be present by virtue of the nature and existence of the Creation.

The second point is that Corbett sees ideological statements as being 'designed' to condition men socially. It is not the 'ordinary man' who gains by them, but the crafty ideologist and his masters. Thus the ideologist's motives are as suspect as his logic. But Corbett has misunderstood the kind of relationship that exists between the ideologist's aims and his beliefs. Corbett sees the Catholic or Marxist as believing certain things in order to gain power. He accuses them of believing because they want something. It does not occur to him that they want certain things *because* they believe. The point is that the Catholic may be fully aware of all the things that may happen to someone who does not have a therapeutic abortion, but still be unable to sanction such an operation because the outcome (the loss of the unborn child) cannot be seen as a good thing whatever else happens. 'The facts' do not refute what the Catholic believes since it is what the Catholic believes that determines the moral significance of the facts. Corbett is right to suggest that there are no ultimate grounds on which the Catholic or Marxist may demonstrate the objective nature of his beliefs (the same, incidentally being true of his own beliefs), but it does not follow from this that they are strictly comparable.

The similar claim to that made by Corbett advanced by MacIntyre is that Christianity is an ideology, but one that has drained itself of any empirical content.[15] The replacements offered by an increasingly secular, and, it seems, neurotic society – on the one hand Marxism, on the other psycho-analysis – have failed to fill the gap left by belief in God and we are left to search for a more satisfactory ideological replacement. MacIntyre writes:

> Against those who still believe that some particular ideology is still able to provide the light that our social and individual lives need, I shall assert that – in the case of Christianity, of Psychoanalysis and above all, of Marxism – either intellectual failure, or failure to express the forms of thought and action which constitute our contemporary social life, or both, have led to their necessary and in the long run not to be regretted decay.[16]

Now, as Henry Drucker has pointed out,[17] it is difficult to see the way in which psychoanalysis is an ideology in the way that Marxism, nationalism and liberalism are. Certainly in terms of vocal manifestations in the political arena there is no parallel to be drawn. If we wish to call psychoanalysis ideological, it would certainly have to be distinguished from those ideologies named above.

However, more needs to be said about MacIntyre's claim than this. It is clear from MacIntyre's comment that he thinks that Marxism and Christianity are similar (in the logic of the discourse that they employ) and that Christianity has now been replaced by Marxism as a more recent if not more advanced form of ideological commitment. In order to establish this claim, he has to show that they are related by something more than historical contingency.

It might be claimed that mankind has progressed from primitive myths and magic to religion, replacing notions of gods that are in trees or animals with that of a God who does not inhabit in person the world he created, and that the next stage in this development is the abandonment of religion for a yet more sophisticated view, namely, ideology.[18] But the theological writings of Aquinas or Augustine, whatever failings they do have, are as accomplished as Mill's or Marx's contribution to their respective traditions. Indeed, when compared to Aquinas, the writings of national socialism and fascism in particular (two ideologies peculiar to the twentieth century) seem unsophisticated in MacIntyre's terms. His view only makes sense if we have a one-dimensional picture of human understanding; the sort of perspective that sees the parting of the Red Sea as the precursor of the Hoover Dam, or a magical rite as an attempt to perform a scientific experiment. It is this kind of assumption that permeates the anthropological writings of Sir James Frazer, and is powerfully exposed by Wittgenstein in some remarks on Frazer's *The Golden Bough*.[19] In particular, Wittgenstein notes that the people Frazer describes already understood causal connections; magical rites were an *expression* of something important, not the deployment of a causal hypothesis.[20] Why, for example, should they pray for rain at the start of the rainy season? Surely, if prayers were thought to have a mysterious causal efficacy, it would be sensible to pray at the start of the dry season! In this context it is worth recalling G. K. Chesterton's remark when told that the presence of food and wine in an Egyptian tomb 'proved' that the Egyptians *must* have believed that the dead were capable of eating and drinking; he said that this conclusion no more followed from the evidence than the fact that Christians put flowers on a grave 'proved' that they *must* believe that the dead can both see and smell!

Before going on to look at the parallels that might be drawn between religion and ideology it is as well to draw a distinction between theology and the philosophy of religion. This is not easy; as D. Z. Phillips points out, it is rather like working on the Tower of Babel with the added disadvantage of there being no convenient agreement as to the object of the project.[21] Nevertheless, some general remarks can be made. Theology is the systematic attempt by which the believer shows, as Aquinas put it, 'God in His Godhead'. The theologian does this in a variety of ways, by examining the scriptural conception of God, by examining what the Councils of the Church have said, or by asking questions such as 'can the number six be the Creator?'. The important thing to note is the relationship between theology and faith. St Anselm, for example, described his work as that of 'faith seeking understanding', and of himself as 'believing that I might understand'. Faith here is an *inner* demand of theology. That is, theology may be separate from the other facets of religion, but not from religion itself. It is not, in this sense, separate from the beliefs that it expresses; for it is not a ground for belief, it is a systematic, doctrinal, expression *of* that belief, in the way that public worship is the liturgical expression of that belief. The theologian must always be within a religious tradition. Contrary then, to the assertion made at the start of Chapter 2 of *Honest to God*[22] by John Robinson, traditional theology is not based on the five proofs of God's existence offered by Aquinas, but on faith in God's word as revealed in scripture. It is worth noting in this context that the *Summa Theologia* does not *start* with or from (in the sense of being *based* upon) the Five Ways at all.[23] Secondly, though we may examine (and find wanting) the arguments put forward by Aquinas for their philosophical coherence as proofs, it is not clear that they were intended as such. Who were the thirteenth-century atheists to whom Aquinas could have been addressing himself?

Having said all this, it ought to be clear, on the one hand, that the theologian is not an impartial judge between the claims advanced by two churches or within different religious traditions, but a man committed to a religious stance. The philosopher of religion is, on the other hand, concerned with the logic of religious statements, not, *qua* philosopher, choosing between them. The philosophy of religion is not faith seeking understanding; it is concerned with what is involved in belief, rather than expressing it. In this sense the philosopher sees the philosophical relevance of certain concepts, but not their religious significance (which is not the same as their significance for religion): for in one sense, to understand the religious point of a doctrine *is* to believe in it. Or, to put it the other way around, to believe in a doctrine is to see the religious point of it.[24] If the above characterisation is correct it is clear that the difference between Christianity and Marxism (to keep to MacIntyre's example) cannot be expressed merely by enumerating a series of propositions that one assents to and the other does not. To do so would be to place faith on top, rather than at the heart, of the theologian's task. It would reduce faith to an intellectual extra that could be added on to the end of the liberal or Marxist account of religious experience.

If the foregoing discussion has established the relationship between theology and religion, we are now in a position to draw the correct distinction between ideology and religion that was hinted at earlier in noting the attempt of ideologists to ground their beliefs in what is claimed to be social science or social philosophy. The Christian does not attempt to *ground* his belief in the theology let alone in a secular discipline like philosophy or science. On the contrary, it is those very beliefs that make theology possible. To labour the point, theology does not stand below or outside of belief (whatever your metaphorical preference) as a foundation based on 'the facts'; it is itself another way of expressing those beliefs. If the relationship, for example, between Marxism and history were of the same type as that between theology and religion, it would produce for the Marxist the

Ideology and Religion

extremely unsatisfactory spectacle of Marxism appealing for verification to a version of itself: the claims of the ideologist and theologian are, I suggest, different.

Now we can, of course, argue with MacIntyre that both claims are mistaken and in the end vacuous. But it is important to see that, even if this were so, the mistakes of the ideologist and of the religious believer are of a different order. The desire to organise the state in accordance with the laws of God may produce disastrous results, as the Anabaptists found out, but though such a society might be strange and unpleasant, it could only be unstable, not an impossibility. Again appealing to the Bible might not demonstrate that only theocratic government is legitimate, but it is not the same kind of mistake as trying to base the political structure of a society on the discoveries of natural science. The appeal to a religious authority may prove contingently unacceptable, but it will not be incoherent as an appeal to science must invariably prove to be.

Even if it is accepted that the forms of an ideological and of a religious work are different, it might still be claimed that the content or practical achievement is the same, or amounts to the same thing. By content or practical achievement I do not mean a series of propositions that are affirmed by either or both, or even their respective ontologies, but something more akin to the fact that religion and ideology both offer a 'world view'. One similarity that can be noted is the radical discontinuity that exists between our previous standards and those we now adopt when we become religious believers or adherents of an ideology. The world then becomes, in an important sense, a different place and we characterise such a metanoia in terms such as 'dying to the world', 'being reborn', or recognising 'alienation' and escaping 'false consciousness'. In saying this the believer and adherent are not claiming to have *more information* about the world than they did before, but that they see it as it 'really is'. That is, they claim to see the *real* significance of events; to have gone beyond mere appearances. This is connected with the fact that, in adopting a religious or ideological standpoint, the individual is rescued from insignificance and placed at the centre of the stage. No one is insignificant in the sight of God, and each 'proletarian' has a part to play in securing the success of the 'revolution'. And, as in a Shakespearian tragedy, nothing, when seen from the total scheme of things, is irrelevant or insignificant. A person may hold to moral standards and yet still say that 'life has no meaning' or 'life is a mystery', but the believer and adherent are committed to saying that life is meaningful, and that through salvation, class struggle, or national self-determination, the value and intelligibility of their life is revealed. For the man of conviction there is a point to life the significance of which is not immediately given in experience. This significance will, of course, be different, depending on the faith or ideology embraced. What the Marxist sees as a symptom of the class structure of society may appear to the liberal or conservative as evidence that the rule of law is being upheld against the claims of sectional interests. The point is that both the believer and the adherent see all events as peculiarly significant within their respective frameworks. Nothing is excluded.

But to say that Christians, Marxists, liberals and nationalists all find events significant within a certain framework will not get us very far, unless we can look at the kind of significance involved. One way of trying to bring out the parallel it is claimed exists between them is to look at the way that holding a 'world-view' helps a person to work towards a goal. In the case of the Christian this can be put roughly as follows. The kingdom of God is not (only) the final stage of history, but the trajectory of history. The fact that the kingdom will come, or rather the fact that the kingdom has been established, though not fulfilled, enables us to work towards salvation. This is to say that the kingdom of God is not just the top note of the ascending musical scale of history, but the trajectory of history. In a similar way, it is the belief in the certainty of the 'proletarian revolution' that provides, for the Marxist, the significance of history, and enables him to see himself as advancing a cause. It was the 'correct' attitude taken by the Bolshevik faction to the 'bourgeois revolution' in Russia (that is, of seeing it as the prelude to, and midwife of, the 'proletarian revolution') which could be seen to justify their tolerance of liberals, whilst perceiving in this convenience the deeper dimension necessary for their eventual 'success'.

But we should not, like Corbett, get carried away with similarities that exist only on the surface. For the Christian, the post-Resurrection world of the eschatological perspective is one in which the certainty of the kingdom is assured. Even if the world were to end tomorrow, then this would not negate what the Christian sees as the victory of Christ over sin and death, since the event that assures this victory has been revealed to him through his faith and is guaranteed by it. It cannot be reversed by a future event. There is, it must be admitted, a serious disagreement over the *kind* of event the Resurrection was, and whether or not claims about its occurrence are potentially falsifiable by *historical* evidence. On one side of the dispute is the unlikely, if not unholy, alliance between Catholic natural theologians and sceptics, such as Antony Flew, who insist that it is, on a factual level, on a logical par with other historical events. On the other side are modern Protestant theologians, led by Barth and Bultmann, who put it safely outside the bounds of historical investigation.[25] The kind of invulnerability they claim has led to charges of vacuity, reductionism and inconsistency.[26] But such a

Ideology and Religion 33

controversy cannot, I think, alter the contention that to be a Christian is to believe in the occurrence of the Resurrection, and in the Christian faith its occurrence cannot be challenged. However, it is clearly not the case that believing in Marxism similarly guarantees the occurrence of the 'revolution'. As a temporal event the 'revolution' is a possibility, but not a certainty. Marxism cannot preclude the possibility of nuclear energy destroying the world.

Earlier, it was noted that 'authentic' human relationships were inaugurated by the advent of the kingdom of God for the Christian and will be by the coming of the 'revolution' for the Marxist. Again, it is worth examining what is involved in these concepts of authenticity, and seeing if there are any significant disparities. One which comes to mind is that for the Marxist (or indeed, any ideologist) authentic human history is still history. It is still within the bounds of time in which it is possible that men perform actions, catch colds and die. For the Christian, this is not so; for whatever we are to make of the notion of eternal life, it cannot be a temporal duration. Our salvation is not an event. It is outside time, and without all that occurs in time. To say that there will be no colds or deaths in heaven is to make a grammatical remark, and not to comment on the superiority of preventive medicine there.

This brings us to the notion of the eternal, and its importance in religious life. It is a difficult notion, especially when connected to questions about survival after death, and I do not want to comment on the complex issues involved. I shall only consider the relationship between the eternal and temporal and try to make clear their incompatibility. There is a danger of looking on the after-life as being like the last reel of a Western movie – that is, the time following the time of reckoning when the divine sheriff gives to everyone their just deserts. If we thus look on eternity as a period to be added on to the end of history this must preclude our making the essential distinction we have to make in order to grasp the point made by D. Z. Phillips in advancing the following two quotations.[27] The first is from Antony Flew, the second from Wittgenstein. Flew says:

> And if this future life is supposed to last forever, then the question of whether or not it is fictitious ... is of overwhelming importance. For what are three score years and ten compared with all eternity?[28]

Here eternity is seen as more time. What Phillips wants to stress is the qualitative difference the use of the term eternal makes, hence the following passage from the *Tractatus*:

> Not only is there no guarantee of the temporal immortality of the human soul, that is to say, of its eternal survival after death; but

in any case the assumption fails to accomplish the purpose for which it has always been intended. Or is some riddle solved by my surviving for ever? Is not this eternal life as much of a riddle as our present life? The solution of the riddle of life in space and time lies *outside* space and time.²⁹

The point Phillips is making is that to ask 'how long does eternity last?' is as pointless as asking 'where do parallel lines meet?' or 'what is the largest number in an infinite series?'.

Seeing the grammatical distinction between eternity and temporality helps us to draw one final distinction in this area. It is related to the earlier discussion of the past and future. The Marxist may see the General Strike of 1926 as a *defeat* for the working-class movement in Britain, a defeat that will be reversed by future events. The working-class may receive setbacks but in the end it will be victorious. For the Christian, on the other hand, the Crucifixion cannot be understood in this way. It was not a defeat that will be overcome at a later date, or even a defeat that will come to be seen as essential to the final victory. Seen from the standpoint of the eternal, it always is a victory. As Kierkegaard puts it:

> nothing in the world has even been so completely lost as was Christianity at the time that Christ was crucified . . . never in the world had anyone accomplished so little by the sacrifice of a consecrated life as did Jesus Christ. And yet in this same instant, eternally understood, He had accomplished all . . . Was it not said by many intelligent men and women, 'The result shows that He has been hunting after phantasies; He should have married. In this way He would now be a distinguished teacher in Israel.'
>
> And yet, eternally understood, the crucified one had in the same moment accomplished all! But the view of the moment and the view of eternity . . . have never stood in such atrocious opposition. It can never be repeated. This could only happen to Him. Yet eternally understood, He had in the same moment accomplished all and on that account, said, with eternity's wisdom 'It is finished'.³⁰

So far I have tried to show that there are important differences between both the form and content of religious and ideological claims. In particular, that theology is not a *ground* for Christianity, as history or science are claimed to be a ground for Marxism, and that the eternal (as understood by Christians) is a category that has no equivalent in ideological writings. I want to conclude by making some remarks about religious practices and ideologically inspired activities.

When we consider religious practices, there are important differences even within Christianity. The mass, with its attendant notions of sacrament and priesthood, is a central feature of Roman Catholicism and yet it is regarded by extreme Protestant sects as 'a blasphemous fable and dangerous deceit'. The notions of sacrament and priesthood are not to be found in the religious talk of the Pentecostal sects and the Quakers. Are, then, the differences between Christian sects greater than, or of a different order from, the differences between religious and 'ideological' practices? It might be argued, for example, that the 'Internationale' and 'Tomorrow Belongs to Me' are the equivalent of 'Onward Christian Soldiers' or 'Full in the Panting Heart of Rome'; that 'A letter Concerning Toleration' is similar to a Papal Encyclical, and that the devotion shown by Catholics to St Francis is echoed by that shown by the Russians to Lenin and the Chinese to Mao. The monument to Mao is certainly as grand as that accorded to any Christian saint.

There are, of course, similarities, just as there are between revivalist meetings and football matches or rock concerts. Even so, it is important to see that calling Russian devotion to Lenin 'religious' is not to be taken literally, and that such usage is parasitic on authentic religious notions. In seeing the part a notion plays in a way of life, it is essential to put it into the appropriate context. The context for religious ideas, such as prayer and worship, is that of religion itself, where the notion of what is sacred and holy and the conception of God all determine the sense that prayer has for the believer, and the very possibility of praying. The context in which ideological activities and pronouncements take place is a different one, with different conceptions providing different possibilities. It is illegitimate to 'abstract' notions from the two contexts and say that they really amount to the same thing. It would be as absurd as equating a Saturday night dance in Pitscottie with an African ritual for choosing a wife on the grounds that there is music, dancing, possibly the use of hallucinatory substances, and that the end result is the same – people pair off into couples. Seen within their appropriate contexts, we can see that the concepts which give life to one are absent from the other. Thus it would be mistaken to equate prayers that are tied to the notion of an Eternal God with whatever regard the Chinese have for Mao when the notion of eternity has no place in Maoism. To this extent, there are no ideological equivalents of prayers and worship at all. In a similar way religious rituals and their expression are distinct from ideological rituals. Again, it would be no use arguing that the notions of the sacred and holy only make a difference of degree, for they are what make religious notions religious. In this sense they are *internal* to the religious notion of a ritual, and once this is seen we should not make the mistake of equating religious and ideological practices on the grounds of *external* similarities.

NOTES: CHAPTER 2

1 P. Corbett, *Ideologies* (Hutchinson, London, 1965), p. 58.
2 D. Raphael, *Problems of Political Philosophy* (Macmillan, London, 1970), p. 17. It is not entirely clear whether he means that ideologies are non-rational or irrational. I suspect the latter.
3 Francis Barker, 'The morality of knowledge and the disappearance of God', *New Blackfriars*, September 1976, pp. 403–15. Marxists believe that *all* religions are ideological, I shall only be concerned with Christianity in this chapter.
4 Not all liberals are anti-theological, T. H. Green for example.
5 Amos 2: 6–7; Micah 6: 8; Isaiah 1: 11–18.
6 Matthew 25: 21–6.
7 Schleiermacher held that there was a specific, identifiable, religious experience, correctly apprehended by the believer and misconceived by the atheist. This buys exemption from the atheists' criticisms (as I, and only I can know the quality of this experience); but if the experience is private in this Cartesian sense, it is difficult to see how the atheist can be accused of unfairly rejecting claims made for it. If it is not private, Schleiermacher ought to admit the possibility of something other than this inner feeling being used to test whether or not it is a sign of the divine, and this must apply to *his own* inner feelings.
8 Marx may not have been bothered about 'proving' the falsity of religion as he thought that this would have been as irrelevant as giving a drug addict lectures on the harm of drug-taking. Religion would not disappear through argument, but only when certain social conditions had been removed.
9 For example, Robert Tucker's account of Marxism in R. Tucker, *The Marxian Revolutionary Idea* (Allen & Unwin, London, 1970).
10 When asked to sum up the four volumes of 'Church Dogmatics', Barth replied 'Jesus loves me, this I know, for the Bible tells me so'.
11 Patrick Corbett, *Ideologies* (Hutchinson, London, 1965).
12 Alasdair MacIntyre, *Against the Self-Images of the Age* (Duckworth, London, 1971). Hereafter referred to as *ASIA*.
13 ibid., pp. 117–18.
14 ibid., p. 118.
15 See also *The Religious Significance of Atheism* (written with Paul Ricoeur).
16 *ASIA*, p. viii.
17 Henry Drucker, *The Political Uses of Ideology* (Macmillan, for the LSE, London, 1974), pp. 97–8.
18 cf. Compte's idea of progression from theology to science via metaphysics.
19 L. Wittgenstein, 'Remarks on Frazer's *Golden Bough*, *The Human World*, May 1971, p. 95.
20 This is not to say that they can *never* be mistaken in this way, but that they need not be so.
21 D. Z. Phillips, *The Concept of Prayer* (Routledge & Kegan Paul, London, 1965).

22 J. A. T. Robinson, *Honest to God* (Westminster, London 1963), p. 29.
23 Question 1 is entitled 'On what sort of teaching Christian theology is and what it covers'.
24 This should not be confused with the claim that belief is necessary for understanding *tout court*. A person may understand what is involved in the doctrine of the Trinity and reject it. My claim is that seeing the point of an activity is not the same as knowing what constitutes a valid move within it or defending it against objections.
25 Bultmann puts the point as follows: 'It is precisely its immunity from proof which secures the Christian proclamation against the charge of being mythological.' *Kerygma and Myth, A Theological Debate*, rev. and trans. R. H. Fuller (Harper & Row, New York, 1961), p. 44.
26 See A. MacIntyre 'The religious significance of atheism' and 'God and the theologians' (reprinted in *ASIA*). For some interesting and pertinent criticisms of Bultmann, see R. W. Hepburn, 'Demythologizing and the problems of validity', in *New Essays in Philosophical Theology*, ed. A. G. N. Flew and A. MacIntyre (Macmillan, London, 1964).
27 D. Z. Phillips, *Death and Immortality* (Macmillan, London, 1970), pp. 48–9.
28 A. G. N. Flew, op. cit.
29 L. Wittgenstein, *Tractatus Logico-Philosophicus* (Routledge & Kegan Paul, London, 1961), 6.4312.
30 S. Kierkegaard, *Purity of Heart*, trans. D. V. Steere (Harper, New York, 1956), pp. 120–1.

3
Ideology and Philosophy

In this introduction to a book of essays on ideology and philosophy[1] Alasdair MacIntyre anticipates the making of certain objections to his enterprise, expecting that 'almost everybody . . . will find grounds for quarrelling with the way in which [he has] tried to carry out this project'.[2] However, with the project generally defined in the claim that the unity of his book 'resides . . . in the aspiration to link philosophical criticism and ideological commitment', he supposes that 'doubtless . . . very few will be found to quarrel'.[3] I should like to consider, though not in any quarrelsome spirit, what MacIntyre's aspiration amounts to; that is, I shall examine what he takes his task to involve and will not be directly concerned with the adequacy of his performance. In so far as a reader is unclear about the aims of the book, he is in no position to judge the writer's achievement. In any case, MacIntyre specifically disclaims knowing how to tie his 'arguments together into a substantive whole'.[4] Since we are not being offered a consistent and harmonious whole but rather a variety of essays that 'do not provide anything approaching a unified and systematic treatment',[5] any assessment of the book must be peculiarly circumspect. Given the avowedly fragmentary and tentative nature of even the philosophical essays, to say nothing of the book reviews, the difficulty for the reader is at least twofold: to see the essays as representing 'stages in a single inquiry', and to appreciate the bearing of certain discussions in moral philosophy and the philosophy of action on ideology.[6]

One may begin by considering together both the general introduction and the introduction to Part Two, for here we may expect to find not only clues regarding the unity of the book and the features of the single inquiry, but also the nearest approach to a 'unified and systematic' view, however compressed, of MacIntyre's project. In addition, Chapter 1 provides a perspective of some generality since it contains a discussion of 'what we ought to understand by the expression "ideology" '.[7] In particular I shall pay some attention to the claim that 'a good deal of ideology not only overlaps with the proper concerns of philosophy, it *is* philosophy'.[8]

Now, to anticipate certain lines of criticism is certainly not to earn exemption from criticism altogether. Indeed, even if MacIntyre identifies, for the purpose of opposing it, some point one is strongly inclined to make against him, this does not mean that the critic is disarmed. He *may*, of course, give greater weight to the counter-objection than to his own original objection, but the anticipation of his objection does not prevent him making it all the same. However, if a writer has quite clearly anticipated the precise objection that comes to one's mind, appears to appreciate the issues, and yet maintains the position objected to, it may be as well to resist pressing the objection at the outset. Even if one has what appears to be a knock-down argument, there will be cases where employing it on a particular occasion is precisely what prevents one from understanding further. An obvious example would be a student of ethics, struck by the enormity of the 'Naturalistic Fallacy', who could not but consider Mill's treatment of 'desired' and 'desirable', say, as a paradigm instance of the alleged fallacy. And now suppose Mill unfortunate enough to find a defender who could not get past the idea that the real offence lay in the commission of the 'Naturalistic Fallacy'. For any genuine engagement of thought one would need to renounce such knock-down arguments. Not primarily because the opposition insist on wielding counter-arguments in the same manner. There may not be an opposition; rather one's own thought may be torn two ways. If one cannot see past either the big question or the big counter-objection, one has to adopt a different, less dramatic, approach in order to get any further. There may still be room for something like the original objection later in the inquiry; but the mere fact that the critic has not taken the short way, but rather has gone to some trouble *despite* his urge to press the gravest charges, makes an important difference to the nature of the understanding sought. Even if he is still inclined to employ the very words of his initial objection, the objection will be importantly different depending on the place it has in his discussion.

There is nothing mysterious about this feature of critical thought: we are all familiar with the difference between coming to see the absurdities in a philosophical view, and never being in a position to see anything but the absurdities. One might compare the understanding of A, for whom 'squaring the circle' is a paradigm of nonsense because he is satisfied that he has a valid *reductio ad absurdum* proof for a given geometry, with that of B, who never gets past the response, to any mention of 'squaring the circle', that if this is not a nonsense expression, he doesn't know what is. B knows, or thinks he knows, in advance of any proof or discussion, that 'squaring the circle' is one of those things that just cannot be done. If, he argues, one knows the sense of 'square' and the sense of 'circle' one sees that these senses mutually exclude each other. His point might be variously put by: 'squaring the circle' is a nonsensical expression, the idea of it is incoherent or a logical impossibility, one cannot use the words like that without either misusing at least one of them or contradicting oneself. Perhaps it is *because* the constituents of the idea are logically distinct that the idea is bound to be incoherent. If the square and the circle are logically distinct only confusion will follow if one fails to distinguish them in the same respect.

Both A and B would be inclined to use the words 'squaring the circle is nonsense', but each would be using them to make very different objections. And one can imagine someone who is not clear which objection he means to make, or wonders whether A and B are not really 'saying the same thing' and merely citing different reasons for the same alleged incoherence. My chief point, however, is that B, to see *what* A was saying and how a proof, even a *reductio*, was relevant at all, would have to put his initial objection aside and could not return to it except as a rejection of A's view. If there is a genuine issue, and there may not be, it may become particularly necessary for B to distance himself sufficiently from his immediate response in order to consider seriously the view of someone who does not appear to entertain the least suspicion that he is dealing in nonsense but devotes himself to the search for a method for doing what both A and B hold to be impossible.

Such criticism as I have to offer of MacIntyre's project is itself liable to be misunderstood unless due attention is paid to the analogies between the effort B might make to achieve a proper distance from his initial reaction so that space is created for genuine inquiry as opposed to the mere clash of positions, and the problem I find in giving a fair account of a task concerning which I very soon and very often want to ask 'what can he be up to?' B's response to 'circle-squaring' is a very natural one: what can a 'circle-squarer' be up to and how can he fail to know that 'squaring the circle' is one of the things that cannot be done? The geometry of the square is one thing and that of the circle another. A thought that is only slightly less compelling may run: what could it be to link philosophical criticism and ideological commitment? How can MacIntyre fail to recognise distinctions both between philosophy and ideology and between criticism and commitment? – distinctions such that no link worth speaking of can be made.

I shall attempt to develop such a line of thought first in order to see at what points it may provide satisfactory criticism of MacIntyre's conception of his task. Whether criticism is satisfactory or not is, I take it, less to do with the extent to which one supposes the author can or should be able to answer the critic's questions and handle his objections, than with whether the critic does justice to the work,

Ideology and Philosophy 41

giving the important issues the attention they deserve and taking care not to distort them. I am supposing that there is something that one finds *worth* criticising, but it need not be part of one's concern to improve the author's argument and to perform the task more adequately. It is certainly no concern of mine.

If one starts with the idea that there are distinctions which MacIntyre may be failing to recognise, it matters very much just what these distinctions amount to and what is supposed to be achieved by employing them. Put another way, when is not recognising a distinction a failure? MacIntyre candidly admits that:

> These essays would normally not be expected to appear within the same covers; for the intellectual habits of the age would construe them as belonging to two different and not very closely related genres.[9]

He makes no apology for this, since one aim of the book is precisely to break with some of these habits. For the purpose of opposing it, he identifies a dichotomy within which we habitually think:

> that between the detailed, analytical, conceptual inquiries of contemporary philosophy and those inquiries into the truth of *Weltanschauungen* which laymen sometimes suppose to be the province of philosophy, but which are so seldom carried on within its bounds.[10]

Now it may well be that it is merely habit that keeps separate these different sorts of inquiries. An analytic philosopher just may not be interested in which *Weltanschauungen* are true, the detailed conceptual inquiry is into the sense in which a *Weltanschauungen* may be said to be true. MacIntyre, in characterising the issue as one of habit, is not dissolving, ignoring, or failing to recognise distinctions between these questions and inquiries. His opposition to the dichotomy involves the view not that there is no distinction between the inquiries but that keeping them separate renders each vulnerable; philosophy to scholasticism and doctrines to intellectual complacency. Each can be made more adequate when linked to the other. Of course, it is not philosophical inquiry and ideological commitment as such that MacIntyre aspires to link. For he believes that 'the nature of contemporary academic philosophy in the Anglo-Saxon world has contributed in a marked way to the persistence among us of certain uncriticised ideological concepts and values'.[11] Most philosophy, it is claimed, is already linked to some ideological concepts and values; it is MacIntyre's view that the philosophy is inadequate on account of its narrowness:

[we may confer] necessity, inevitability, and universality on some conceptual scheme, some way of looking at the world which is in fact local in both time and place and to which there are alternatives. In doing this, philosophy may thus appear to guarantee one way of looking at the world by seeming to demonstrate its necessity; and this is the key role of inadequate philosophy in underpinning ideology.[12]

And that conceptual schemes are inadequate and impoverished if not informed by philosophical knowledge; understanding the world better, 'depends upon the outcome of inquiry in moral philosophy and the philosophy of the social sciences'.[13]

It is useless linking commitment to the failed ideologies of Christianity, psycho-analysis and Marxism to philosophical criticism. For it is precisely philosophical criticism that has revealed their inadequacies in Part One of MacIntyre's book. The philosophical inquiry in Part Two is presented as a necessary condition for a more adequate ideology of the future.

The idea is not simply that those engaged in the ideological disputes of the age have cared too little for rigour and for truth, so that MacIntyre is attempting to make possible a general raising of intellectual standards in ideological debate. Though he is at least making a demand that any doctrine 'expose its vulnerable commitments in all their piecemeal detail',[14] MacIntyre's long-term aim is to contribute to the creation of a 'genuinely post-Marxist ideology of liberation'.[15] Perhaps too much weight should not be put on this particular description. After all, any ideology, for MacIntyre, contains a vision of human liberation, and the demand that the new understanding be post-Marxist is perhaps little more than the demand that it be intellectually respectable, given MacIntyre's judgement that Marxism itself is inadequate because it does not deal with certain philosophical questions, and that any other view is merely clutching at 'fragments of that pre-Marxist moralising which Marx criticised radically and so effectively'.[16]

So it might look as if MacIntyre believes that greater concern for truth and rigour, and the availability of certain philosophical results, should produce some one dominant ideology, but we could not know any of its positive content at least until the philosophical work was reasonably complete. Unfortunately there is a disappointing vagueness here. When questions about the meanings of the key evaluative words have been resolved, we may turn to the 'key question for ideology – whether we (still) possess a language in which we can say what we sometimes desperately want to be able to say.'[17] How would this question be 'answered', even if there were philosophical agreement about the nature of moral judgement, the relation between fact and value, and so on? And is a key question for ideology the same as a key question for those attempting to create a new ideology? One puzzling passage contains the curious sentence:

> If moral considerations are important, if socialism is to have a human face, then we shall have to understand what part reasoning and deliberation play in bringing about one sort of action rather than another.[18]

Taken together with the previously formulated questions – what is morality? and what is its power in the world? – the first conditional presumably means 'if a moral critique can have real effects in the world', if moral talk is more than a smoke-screen or a sham. Yet it appears from the structure of the sentence that MacIntyre intends the second conditional to be equivalent to the first; in a parallel construction three paragraphs earlier he writes after the question 'what is morality? and what is its power in the world?':

> If we are to escape that 'worship of the established fact' that is embodied in the end-of-ideology view of the world, if we are to criticise effectively the world, if we are to criticise effectively the uncontrolled destructive progress of advanced societies in the name of an alternative vision of human liberation – if, *that is* we are to create a genuinely post-Marxist ideology of liberation . . .[19] (my italics)

So, finding that we still possess a substantial moral language, that moral considerations are important, is, somehow, to find that socialism can have a human face. As if the only possibilities were either the (presumably) ineffective criticism of empty moralising, the uncritical 'worship of the established fact'; or, pending the resolution of the crucial problems concerning ethics and action, the hoped-for effective criticism given by humanistic socialism. It is strange that it does not seem to occur to MacIntyre that different people may 'desperately want to be able to say', and indeed *say*, a wide variety of things. There seems to me to be no particular reason why our finding a less corrupt and opaque language in the future should not go with several more or less exclusive ways of understanding the world. Socialism, albeit with a human face, might be advocated, resisted, found morally uninteresting; not only might substantial critical judgements conflict with other genuine judgements, in some moral views social critiques might be of great importance, in others the only critical judgement that mattered might be that exercised on one's own actions alone, those of others being regarded quite differently. Only if MacIntyre's frequent use of 'we' were understood as meaning 'we socialists with humanitarian concerns', would his reference to socialism be intelligible. Yet, clearly, he takes his audience to be professional philosophers and 'all those who have a stake, whether they know it or not, in the outcome of the ideological debates'.[20] I am not sure whom MacIntyre thinks this last formulation leaves out, but one may be confident that more than a few of these will be either committed to some other ideology or 'confidently believe themselves exempt from from ideological adherence'.[21]

My objection here is to the shift from the initial description of MacIntyre's task as one of arguing that 'an ability to understand the world in more adequate and less impoverished ways depends upon the outcome of inquiry in moral philosophy and the philosophy of the social sciences',[22] to his later presentation of the issue as if *one* way of understanding stood particularly to gain from incorporating philosophical results. It is unclear how far MacIntyre seriously thinks that this way must be the ideology of socialism with a human face. One might pass over the juxtaposition of the clauses: 'If moral considerations are important, if socialism is to have a human face . . .'[23] as a piece of carelessness or rhetoric. I have considered it to be of some possible importance as an indication of a shift or uncertainty in MacIntyre's thinking. There appears to be a further uncertainty in what MacIntyre takes himself to be aiming for, when he writes that a philosophical account of actions, reasons and causes is required if 'empirical investigation' is to proceed successfully.[24] A powerful philosophical objection would be that MacIntyre is begging the question of whether any philosophical account of reasons for action would give the same kind of role to 'empirical investigation'. If one says 'the empirical investigation of *these* questions', one is supposing one already knows which questions are to be settled by empirical investigation and is thus already committed to one philosophical view rather than another. Not only is it no objection to a philosophical account, it may be counted as a merit that it leaves entirely obscure what empirical investigation of the questions dealt with would look like. MacIntyre's initial question, 'what part reasoning and deliberation play in bringing about one sort of action rather than another', is raised for him by the fact that a certain Marxist theory draws a contrast between acting in two kinds of ways and makes claims about the conditions in which they are possible. MacIntyre's interest in empirical investigation is an expression of a desire to test these theoretical claims. A philosophical account is required for empirical investigation to proceed successfully. But not any philosophical account will perform the task of helping empirical investigations along. What is required is just the sort of account that can be pressed into service so that empirical investigation may 'proceed successfully'. This means, one supposes, successfully putting the theoretical claims of Marx and Engels to tests of confirmation and falsification.

Now either, as I have suggested, MacIntyre is already committed to one kind of account, or he has an idea of the kind of account he needs if empirical inquiry is to be advanced. Certain outcomes of philosophical inquiry will be useless to meet his requirements. A philosophical account according to which psychology is 'barren', its empirical investigations vitiated by conceptual confusion, may be useless for an aspiring psychologist who wishes to perform successful experimental work.[25] But that is no reason for considering it to be inadequate philosophy. Considering it as a contribution to philosophy has nothing to do with its adequacy as a handbook for psychologists. It may, precisely because of the care for rigour and for truth that it exhibits, be peculiarly recalcitrant material in the hands of someone attempting to conduct empirical investigations or create an alternative vision of human liberation, or of anything else, on the strength of philosophical results. This point raises important issues about the kind of questioning there is in philosophy to which we must return. First, however, I shall deal with MacIntyre's conception of the relation between ways of understanding the world and one's place in it, and empirical inquiry into 'particular features of the changing world'.

We are told that the first key feature of an ideology is that 'it attempts to delineate certain general characteristics of nature or society or both, characteristics which do not belong only to particular features of the changing world which can be investigated only by empirical inquiry. So for Christianity the God-created and God maintained character of the world is just such a characteristic . . .'.[26] But in contrasting Christian claims about divine providence with 'claims about historical events in first-century Palestine', MacIntyre appears to be relying upon a contrast between empirical and non-empirical claims in a way that would rule out treating the 'claims' in which general characteristics are delineated as 'not only' empirical. The general 'claims' would not be empirical at all; they would give the form of the world of which only its particular features would be empirical issues. It is important, too, to recognise that not any empirical matter is an appropriate object of empirical *investigation.* Though it is an empirical fact that animals do not talk, this was neither established by investigation nor does it call for any investigation. Again, for one who understands the world as God's creation, it is understood as such whatever facts happen to obtain. 'The world is God's creation' does not express either an empirical or a metaphysical fact; and while it may be thought of as the answer to a question, this is not the same sense of 'question' that is connected with the notion of inquiry. It is not as if anyone has 'found out' that the world is God's creation as the result of an investigation. And if a Marxist understands change as dialectical change, then particular claims he makes may be said to be intelligible in terms of a delineation of certain general characteristics of the world. The latter might be expressed by saying that the world is governed by dialectical laws, but this shows us how he pictures the world in his speculations and reflections; to take his utterance as expressing a 'claim' or *'statement about* the nature of things' is to make no distinction between ideology, thus far characterised, and metaphysical inquiry.

Not only will those philosophers who take themselves to be engaged in a general inquiry into what there is and how it is to be characterised turn out to be ideologists on this definition, but those who ask questions about statements, their status, truth-conditions, logical relationships, and so forth, will be surprised to be told that this part of the philosophical enterprise not only overlaps with, but *is* ideology, when the statements concerned are those of a particular ideology. Put the other way, MacIntyre takes himself to have shown that 'a good deal of what [he has] characterised as ideology not only overlaps with the proper concerns of philosophy, it *is* philosophy'.[27]

One may either agree that this has indeed been shown in the sense that it follows from the defining characterisation of ideology given; accepting the definition commits one to accepting the consequence. Or one may argue that in any other sense of 'shown', we have not been shown any good reason for accepting that a good deal of ideology is philosophy. I am not sure which response to make since I am not clear how MacIntyre intends us to take his use of 'shown' here. Perhaps it does not matter since strong objections can be made *whether or not* one considers MacIntyre's reasoning to be adequate.

I think there is a sound inference from the given definition to the conclusion that much ideology is philosophy, on *this* characterisation of ideology. And that just means that much ideology is philosophy for anyone accepting the definition (or that part of the definition from which the inference is drawn). But, not only have we been given no reason for accepting this particular definition, one might be strongly inclined to the view that precisely the soundness of the inference is a good reason for rejecting the definition. The argument is accepted, but only as a *reductio ad absurdum.* What is successfully shown is that this is *not* what we ought to mean by the expression 'ideology'.

This supposes that there is something unsatisfactory about the less restricted conclusion: namely, that some ideology is philosophy. One would not treat an argument from a given definition of A to the conclusion that 'some A is defined as B', as a *reductio* unless one objected to 'some A is B'. Let us turn from 'accepting' the definition as the premise of a *reductio* the soundness of which is not in question,

Ideology and Philosophy 47

to a criticism of the definition and a questioning of the soundness of the assumptions made in the course of its formulation.

Thus far I have raised doubts about supposing that characterising the world in a general way amounts to making claims about the world. This is for cases where the characterisation shows how the speaker understands the world, or the form his world has. I have left it an open question whether or not we can attach any sense to the notion that we can make statements or claims about, and conduct inquiry into, the nature of things in general. I have suggested that this notion would be one of metaphysical inquiry or speculation. What is one going to call 'metaphysics' if not an account of the most general features of the world? Not only are the claims made by any such account recognisably metaphysical ones on an untendentious and, indeed, common use of the term; more tendentiously, yet today perhaps even more commonly, many philosophers would say that here we recognise philosophy itself. So one objection to MacIntyre's formulation of his definition might run as follows: if one takes what are, in any case, recognisably features of philosophy as defining features of ideology, then it is hardly surprising that a good deal of ideology is philosophy. But this 'result' must be treated as a by-product. For if the argument were designed to establish that much ideology is philosophy, one would be begging the question precisely in selecting those features. While this strikes me as a fair and forceful point one would need to get to closer grips with the detail of MacIntyre's argument if one is not to be left in the dark as to how MacIntyre comes to beg the question, if he does; and if not, what his argument *is* supposed to establish.

There appear to be two sources of trouble that vitiate the argument. From saying, quite acceptably, that, given statements about the nature of things, 'queries can always be raised' about the status and verification of such statements, MacIntyre shifts to the quite different and implausible point that an ideology as well as being an attempt to 'tell us how the world is', is an attempt that is concerned with the status of the original statements, as if the queries that typically arise from the attempt at philosophical understanding already are just the questions that the ideology has set itself to answer.

What might have been a slip is insisted upon in the second part of the definition:

> I am making it a defining property of an ideology that it does not merely tell us how the world is *and* how we ought to act, but is concerned with the bearing of the one upon the other. This involves a concern, explicit or implicit, with the status of statements of moral rules and of statements expressing evaluations.[28]

48 The Form of Ideology

It is these alleged concerns of particular ideologies with the status of their statements that are supposed to show that much ideology is philosophy. This means, I take it, that MacIntyre is supposing that he can use the expression, 'a good deal of ideology' to mean 'good deal of any ideology'. If any ideology has philosophical concerns, then it *is* philosophy. But here lies the second source of trouble.

For MacIntyre introduces his definition as if it will be a definition of 'ideology'; one might expect a parallel definition of philosophy, and, in fact, I have considered the view that his characterisation is too accurate a one of philosophy *rather than* of ideology. But this is to speak as if the terms 'philosophy' and 'ideology' were the same sort of expression. One might inadvertently define the first, thinking one was defining the second. That it makes sense to say 'I thought the ink was black but it turned out to be blue' shows that 'black and blue' are terms of the same kind, in the same range. Both are colour-words but they are different colour-words. It would be senseless to say: 'I thought the ink was black but it turned out to be expensive.' Applying this contrast and bearing in mind that MacIntyre's discussion of what we ought to mean by the expression 'ideology' gives the key feature of *an* ideology, of *any* ideology, one would expect the conclusion to be of the form: a good deal of any or each ideology is philosophy. Perhaps MacIntyre takes his claim to be just this; after all, he speaks of Christianity and Marxism as if each were largely inquiries into metaphysical and (meta-) ethical issues. But even if one thought of Christianity and Marxism as inquiries, why should we think that each has the same object of inquiry as the other, let alone whether it is the same as that of philosophy? So that, if we take an ideology to be concerned with the status of statements about the world and human conduct, either any such statements are the concern of any ideology, or an ideology is concerned with the status of its own statements. Either it seems that there is an inquiry, 'ideology', to which any ideology contributes competing accounts; or the ideology of Christianity is concerned with philosophical queries that it raises, Marxism with the status of its own claims, and so forth. Either the adherent of any ideology is asking the same general questions as the adherent of any other and as a philosopher, whatever his ideological adherence, if he has one; so Christians and Marxists are distinguished in this connection by their different specific answers to the same general questions. Or, the Christian asks the questions of Christian philosophy, the Marxist those of Marxist philosophy and so on. Christian philosophy, which is a considerable part of Christianity, is concerned with the rest of Christian belief:

How for Christianity are claims about divine providence related to claims about historical events in first-century Palestine? How for

Marxism are claims about the dialectic related to claims about the wage-levels of the working-class under industrial capitalism?[29]

Not only has MacIntyre left no space for the unreflective adherent, it is not clear whether he is required to reflect on both these questions and presumably those relating to other understandings of the world, or only on those raised by his own understanding. There are difficulties either way.

The first view makes it appear that there is a single inquiry, ideology, which *qua* inquiry is a recognisable part of the same inquiry as philosophy. But which specific ideology a man is committed to as an inquirer is given by what answers he has. The distinctiveness of his 'position' is the distinctiveness of his answers, not of his questions. The questions show that he is engaged in an ideological/philosophical inquiry; his answers show which ideology he professes. But then it looks as if there should be space for the question: which is his particular philosophy?

MacIntyre never speaks of particular philosophies, only of philosophical inquiry. This is surely right, for while we distinguish particular philosophical views, conceptions, and so on, we have no use for the expression 'a philosophy'. Although its unity may be hard to discern and to give an account of, we talk of philosophy as being one inquiry. Even where we say, for example, that an epistemological inquiry has a different character from a logical one, we still regard epistemology and logic as branches of, or areas within, the same subject.

But if philosophy is treated as one inquiry so that it makes no sense to talk of particular philosophies, how can 'ideology' be treated as a single inquiry and it still make sense to talk of particular ideologies?

If we withdraw the claim that philosophical inquiry makes up a good deal of the inquiry of ideology and restrict ourselves to claims about given ideologies to the effect that a good deal of each is philosophy, then it is hard to know what is being said. It is not even clear what it would mean to say that a good deal of Christianity is theology. Of a given Christian, Marxist or liberal thinker we may attempt an estimate as to how much of his thought is philosophical or theological, and so on. Certainly, to restrict oneself even further to the second view that I characterised in brief as 'to each ideology its own philosophy' really does land one with the problem of trying to give a sense to the expression 'a particular philosophy' – Christian, Marxist, or whatever. And it does not help at all that we do have a perfectly good use for expressions such as 'a particular philosopher', 'a Marxist philosopher', and so on.

Most of MacIntyre's difficulties stem from his tendency to write as if an ideology is an inquiry at all – quite apart from the further questions as to whether it contributes along with other ideologies to a general inquiry of ideology as such, and how philosophical inquiry enters into the picture. The fact that we find questions and answers in an ideology may encourage the mistaken view that on account of this feature they constitute inquiries. Whatever 'inquiries into the truth of *Weltanschauungen*' may look like, they must be distinguished from the *Weltanschauungen* themselves. Asking questions and giving answers takes many forms and one fails to appreciate the distinctiveness of philosophical questioning, the particular sense of 'question' and 'result' in philosophical contexts, if one regards philosophy as a source of 'results' which 'those who have a stake in the outcome of ideological debates' would do well to consult. Placing the emphasis he does on the result of, the outcomes of, philosophical inquiry, MacIntyre is in danger of paying mere lip-service to the standards of rigour and truth that apply in philosophy.[30] What we need to find out to improve our ideological understanding of the world is no criterion for the importance of a philosophical question or result, unless one is halfway to thinking of philosophy as a social service, providing the needful of those groups who think they know enough to make use of it. Even if it were rigour and truth they were after, not any form this pursuit may take amounts to, or even expresses, a proper care for rigour, at least as a philosopher should understand it. MacIntyre seems to think that once we have a philosophical result we can and should disengage from philosophical inquiry and 'apply the result' in the performance of a non-philosophical task. Otherwise, he fears, that 'of the multiplying of distinctions there may turn out to be no end'. So although

> it is extremely important that rigorous attention to analytical detail should not be vitiated by premature attempts to assess the significance of that detail in terms of some larger issue . . . which distinctions are important, can only be assessed in terms of some criteria of larger significance.[31]

Why should one not accept this statement at face-value, and yet reject any assumption, that the larger issues and significance must be (in any sense) ideological? For a philosopher, the first area in which to apply a result is his own philosophical thinking. A philosophical result is a stimulus to the philosophical imagination. That is where its importance lies. Even where the importance *is* thought to extend beyond philosophy, it is not even available to anyone who is not prepared to think his way to it and past it. If a man is thinking seriously about an important philosophical issue, as opposed to making trivial philosophical 'moves', there is *always* 'crucial detailed work' *for him to do* – not 'to be done', as if his colleagues might do it for him. An interesting result gives him more to think about philosophically. it is not a sign for him to stop thinking or something to pass on to those who have not even begun.

Those of us who have a stake in the outcome of ideological debates – perhaps we all do – can still recognise that the outcome of those debates, if any such outcomes emerge, pass into history and are revived only if there is thought to be occasion for new use of old doctrines. Ideological debates are a comparatively modern phenomenon and perhaps we shall not miss much if one day we should learn to get on without them. The same could be said about the 'crucial' philosophical research programmes that MacIntyre thinks are so urgently required.[32] Although he gives one no idea as to when an attempt at ideological assessment of detailed philosophical work is premature, or at what point I recognise any given result as 'the outcome' and so ready for abstraction, MacIntyre's picture is of inquiries which are of general interest so long as results are awaited and only of interest to scholars once an outcome is produced. For if it is the result that is important for a better understanding of the world, why should anyone but a scholar or antiquarian be concerned with the routes by which it was reached and any concern for philosophical truth exhibited on the way? MacIntyre calls Marxism's lack of concern for philosophical truth a snare to be avoided. The thought appears to be that one gets into ideological trouble if one makes philosophical errors or goes ahead without philosophical solutions. But for a philosopher lack of concern for truth already *is* the worst trouble he could be in. Being properly related to the truth is a condition which his entire efforts attempt to sustain because of what it is – *not* on account of any consequences. At any rate, nothing worth distinguishing as philosophy would fail to have this as a central feature.

This last point might be taken together with a remark of Iris Murdoch's: '[moral] philosophy ought to be defended and kept in existence as a pure activity, or fertile area, analogous in importance to unapplied mathematics or pure "useless" historical research . . .',[33] where 'pure' does not mean 'neutral', or 'fertile' mean rich in consequence for other areas of thought and life. While there may be such consequences, *they* do not make it an activity worth engaging in, whatever their 'importance'. MacIntyre does not say that they do so, but only, I think, because he gives one little idea that philosophy *is* worth doing. He writes about it as if it were a tediously long way of getting answers we urgently need for other (important) purposes. One can't help thinking that if reliable computers could produce the 'results' and check them in a flash, we would have been saved a lot of unnecessary bother. If this is a caricature of philosophy (and hardly any of MacIntyre's original work from the journals deserves to be caricatured thus), it is particularly striking that a philosopher of undoubted ability should suggest it so strongly. Perhaps only a travesty of philosophy could be conscripted in MacIntyre's fight against the self-images of the age. That he seems unable to think of the significance of philosophy except in terms of results and consequences shows what power such images can exert on one's critical imagination, and that the idea of philosophical criticism needs a very different treatment.

NOTES: CHAPTER 3

1   A. MacIntyre, *Against the Self-Images of the Age* (Duckworth London, 1971).
2   ibid., p. viii.
3   ibid., p. viii.
4   ibid., p. x.
5   ibid., p. 95.
6   loc. cit.
7   ibid., p. 7.
8   ibid., p. 6.
9   ibid., p. vii.
10 loc. cit.
11 ibid., p. viii.
12 ibid., p. ix.
13 loc. cit.
14 ibid., p. viii.
15 ibid., p. 93.
16 loc. cit.
17 ibid., p. 94.
18 loc. cit.
19 ibid., p. 93.
20 ibid., p. 95.
21 ibid., p. viii.
22 ibid., p. ix.
23 ibid., p. 94.
24 loc. cit.
25 See L. Wittgenstein, *Philosophical Investigations* (Blackwell, Oxford, 1953), especially Part II, xiv.
26 A. MacIntyre, op. cit., pp. 5, 6.
27 ibid., p. 6.
28 loc. cit.
29 loc. cit.
30 ibid., p. 95.
31 ibid., pp. vii–viii.
32 ibid., p. 93.
33 Iris Murdoch, *The Sovereignty of Good* (Routledge & Kegan Paul, London, 1970), p. 76.

4
Ideology and Theoretical Inquiry

For the student of ideology it is unfortunate that his subject matter has not received, in recognised works, the systematic treatment which provides consistency in the use of the term. Many books have been published which speak about ideology, but the problem is that it is very difficult to apprehend the means by which we can assess their various claims against each other. This is not so, for example, in the philosophy of law: Hart may disagree with Austin and Kelsen, and many disagree with Hart, but at least we have a relatively strong grasp upon how the philosophical disagreements are formulated, if not resolved. Here we have a more or less identifiable tradition of philosophical reflection; in the case of ideology we do not have such a luxury. For this reason I have thought it best to avoid, as much as possible, all explicit reference to the literature on ideology. However, in order to indicate the approach that I am adopting I will briefly consider a very popular contribution which proceeds in a different way from this chapter. John Plamenatz, in his book *Ideology*,[1] takes as his subject matter not the reference of the concept 'ideology', but the use of that term by various writers; he then conjectures on the basis of this collection. Now it seems to me to be rather strange that, having been given a subject matter, an author should think that the appropriate method by which to gain knowledge of the subject is to list the various uses that have been made of the term denoting the subject matter. What we are presented with, in effect, is the information that the term 'ideology' had this or that place in X's theories about society, so that what we receive is more or less good exegesis, and more or less orthodox interpretation.

I hold the view that this approach is a blind alley for anyone who sets out to begin an investigation into the nature of ideological thinking, and I shall now explain, very briefly, why I think this is so.[2]

If somebody were to ask me what oxygen is, i.e. what it is that the term 'oxygen' refers to, I would direct him to a science textbook or an authority on the matter. I certainly would not say: 'Go and look at the history of science from the time at which the Phlogiston Theory ceased to command general acceptance.' I would have been asked a scientific question, not a historical one concerning changes in the meaning of a term. The answer to a historical question could never settle the answer to a scientific question precisely because the questions are addressed to different areas of concern, or knowledge. In short: knowledge of the changes in the meaning of a term is not knowledge of the referent of a concept; it is the latter which the scientist seeks in the case of oxygen. The reference of the term 'ideology' might be understood analogously: the term 'ideology' refers to a particular kind of thought. Thought is here taken to be the subject matter of philosophy, and philosophy, broadly conceived, speaks of thought in terms of the conceptual relations which constitute in a logical manner the different areas of thought. If this account of concepts and their reference is valid then how could it be that any philosophical problem about the nature of a certain area of thought, say, ideology, could be advanced one step by giving us a history of the usage of a term? If we want to know about ideology then we shall have to conduct an investigation. If we want to know the meaning of the term in Marx, Mannheim, and so on, then we will be involved in an exegetical exercise. The failure, on the part of Plamenatz, to distinguish exegetically established meaning from reference results in his telling us nothing about ideology; in his work the history of ideas has become, by sleight of hand, a substitute for philosophical inquiry.

In this chapter I shall be concerned to consider one way in which the reference of the term 'ideology' might be established. To do this I will attempt to determine the nature of the supposedly investigatory exercise called 'political theory'. I have concluded that this will prove useful because I hold the view that the terms 'political ideology' and 'political theory' are not synonyms, and it seems to me that an awareness of how we might begin to formulate the differences between their meanings is important. Also, as we shall see, some people have employed what might be termed a sceptical account of political theory in order to give an account of ideological thinking; in this chapter I shall attempt to set some limits to such an employment.

Contributors to political theory have set themselves the task of answering such curious questions as 'what is the state?' and 'under what conditions is the exercise of its powers legitimate?',[3] and they have done so by explanations of its existence, justifications of criticisms of its being maintained and recommendations concerning arrangements for political, or, more broadly, social life. Such a simple statement of the nature of the inquiry engaged in by political theorists does not, of course, say anything of the heterogeneous character of the collection of investigations that have been supposed contributions to that inquiry. But that does not matter; what is relevant is that the various explanations, justifications and recommendations are supposedly part of, or derived from, what I shall term theoretical knowledge or understanding. Thus, in a perfectly legitimate sense, we may ask: what is the object of which we are trying to gain knowledge, such that we can begin to formulate explanations, justifications and recommendations? This object will have to be metaphysically prior to the existence of the state and independent of it, in order, first that the existence of the state may be explained, and, secondly, that the condition under which that object obtains in any one state may be justified or criticised. This object may itself undergo modification, but must always be distinguishable from those arrangements which we call the 'state'. Such a modification is envisaged in German idealism (most notably in Hegel) and in Marxism. For the purposes of this chapter let us call the object of investigation 'human nature'. We may feel justified in calling our supposed knowledge of this object theoretical, because the postulation of the independence of this object from any one state, essential to the notion of a general explanation, implies either a uniformity in the object, or a change in it, specified in the theory, not by recourse to a narrative history of various political associations.

An illustration of my point here can be given by referring to Marxism. One of the characteristics of man, according to Marx, is that his nature is not static, but changes in response to the specific relation it has to nature within a mode of production. To speak dialectically: the history of man is supposed to be the successive self-re-creation of man by himself by means of his productive relationship to nature, a relationship which is itself changed in this process. The alienation suffered by man is due to the particular relation he has to nature, which is determined by the means of production and by the antagonistic relation between those classes engaged in the productive process. Progress in the means of production, i.e. technological progress, and the resolution of the particular antagonism between classes constitutes a change in man's nature. Thus when Marx claims that 'the history of all hitherto existing society is the history of class struggles', then this is a claim derived from his theory of human nature, which has alienation as its central notion.

It is, I think, helpful to label the conceived object of investigation 'human nature', not only because this term is general enough not to cause us problems of classification, but for the reason that it suggests a helpful *analogy* with the reference of the term 'physical nature', which indicates a form of inquiry, where, for example, changes in an organism are explained by physical and chemical theories. In this way we have theoretical knowledge of an organism of the kind which could enable us to list those conditions which lead to its most efficient functioning. This juxtaposition of human nature and physical nature as objects of inquiry is not as absurd as it might intuitively appear to be: if there is to be a theoretical explanation for the existence of the state, as a form of association, and justification or criticism derived from it, then it has to be the case that human nature is a discrete object of investigation. Thus a knowledge of that object will enable us to specify those conditions under which it obtains in its most satisfactory form. Any change in the object would have to be accountable for by the various theories giving us knowledge of the object in terms of its relation to its environment.

I hold the view that this is the only way that political theorists could proceed if what was produced were to be properly theoretical and explanatory. That is to say that while in natural science the notion 'explanation' is conceptually related to prediction and the possibility of technological innovation, so in political theory that notion is conceptually related to justification or criticism of an actual state and the formulation of an intention to act in the political world. For example, the intention to 'bring about socialism' would have as a necessary condition for its formulation a knowledge of Marxist theory.

Such a view concerning political theory does not, I believe, amount to much of methodological importance for the would-be political theorist, and it does not because I have no idea what such an inquiry could consist of; this means that I cannot conceive of how the term 'human nature' could be construed referentially in an analogous way to the term 'physical nature'. I will now give an illustration of the ground of my scepticism concerning political theory by an example making use of the concept of intention. Physical and chemical theories are related to agents' intentions in terms of those theories supplying the knowledge that enables the production of the capability necessary for the achievement of some end. This is a theory–practice relation which I term 'technological'. It is the application of theoretical knowledge in the achievement of some end. Any construction, then, is technological in nature when it enables an agent to bring about a causal sequence intentionally, and when that causal sequence can be explained by the specific physical and chemical theories which were applied in the construction of the relevant technological device(s).

Let us examine the relation between theoretical knowledge and the forming of an intention more closely. We might say that we know the meaning of a statement of intention in an analogous way to grasping the meaning of an assertion, that is that we have fulfilment conditions. However, I think it is necessary to supplement this suggestion: if we want to grasp the meaning of the statement of an intention,

Ideology and Theoretical Inquiry 57

as distinct from an aim, we might say that we have to have a grasp upon the particular capacity that a person has in order to carry out his intention. In the context of a theory–practice relation this will involve a grasp of the theoretical knowledge necessary to the formation of the intention, i.e. a knowledge of what is involved in carrying it out. An illustration of this point can be given by reference to alchemy. An alchemical theory may have given people grounds for thinking that lead could be turned into gold. We see here how certain concepts adduced in the theory relate to the possibility of the forming of a specific intention. Now in order to say of the intention that it is ill-formed we refer to the inadequacy of the theory, not to a fact – in this case that lead cannot be turned into gold – that stands supposedly independent of our argument that the theory is inadequate. This is so because in the context of a theory–practice relation the meanings of terms, that is, what concepts are expressed by them, are specified within the relevant theories. Because meaning is specified here the reference of the term will be partially determined by the theories; that is, have to refer to the theories to establish the reference. In short, to understand the intention we refer to the explanation that would be given of the execution of the intention.

Now the question is: is it possible that political activity could be grounded in some body of theoretical knowledge, in a way *analogous* to a body of scientific knowledge providing us with the capacity to intend to bring about a state of affairs? And the answer must be, I think: no, it is impossible. This can be brought out initially by noticing the difference between the capacity to instigate causal relations, such that the resulting state of affairs is explained by reference to the relevant theoretical knowledge, and the ability to bring about political changes which do not instigate causal relations, but have significance in relation to the actions of men. As we noted, the political theory model implies that some object (human nature) be responsive to these changes. But in what does this response consist, and how do we explain it? The reference to human nature cannot be to the actions of men, because, as we noted above, this would be circular. While the explanation of a causal process presupposes the theoretical knowledge we possess, such that the coming about of a state of affairs is explained, in the explanation of political activity there is no scope for generality just because what we have in mind, when engaging in the explanation of political activity, are the actions of men in relation to the changes they bring about. It is not a relation accountable for in terms of a theoretically determined knowledge under which we subsume objects and their movements.

I will attempt to justify this point by a brief discussion of the nature of scientific understanding. Within this mode, I wish to claim, physical reality is understood by the employment of generalities.

These generalities are established by a peculiar kind of reference to reality called experimentation. An experiment constitutes a distinctive form of reference to the world just in so far as it has universal significance, i.e. its occurrence at a particular point in space and time is irrelevant. The important point here is that an experiment is peculiar in terms of its being a specific kind of reference to reality; it is not a reference to a different kind of reality than physical reality understood in terms of specific natural events in space and time. Nature is not an appearance understood in terms of a reality, but is something straightforwardly identified, for the purpose of explanation, as causal sequences describable by scientific theories.

It is in this sense that scientific laws are not generalisations in that an observer moves from particular observations to a statement, or set of statements, which covers all cases within a class. The procedure of generalisation involves the idea that we move from observed cases to a statement covering unobserved and hypothetical cases, but that these cases and the observed ones have the same logical status. My claim is that the kind of reference to reality postulated in the case of an experiment already has built into it the notion of universality in virtue of the irrelevance of spatio-temporal factors. For example, we may generalise in the context of breakdowns in technology, say, concerning radiator crackings and missile failures, but scientific theories do not speak of 'radiator crackings' and 'missile failures', but of the constituents of these objects, a knowledge of which is specified physically and chemically. My example here is taken from an article by Maurice Mandelbaum[4] where he attacks Hempel's notion of covering laws for attempting to seek regularities of connection between some particular complex type of event and some particular complex set of conditions. Mandelbaum claims, quite correctly in my view, that this is not the procedure in natural science, which does not involve this kind of generalisation but explains by referring what is to be explained to some already given generally stated knowledge.

Another example may be advanced from the realm of organic change – if we were to observe a caterpillar changing into a butterfly we could introduce chemical theories to account for the change, but in doing this we do not understand 'butterfly nature' in terms of physical nature, i.e. what the transition is, for the scientist, is a sequence of chemical changes.

In contrast, the procedure of political theory is quite different. This difference consists of that enterprise positioning two entities: first, human nature and, secondly, those particular practices and conditions – legal, economic, political, religious, and so on – which are constitutive of social life at any particular time and place. These conditions are to be understood in terms of a functional relation to human nature. This proposed relation is, I argue, impossible to make. It is impossible because the assertion of the relation rests upon a conflation of the notions of reduction and subsumption. A scientific theory subsumes in the sense that what is explained is an instance of something generally specified, but the strategy of political theory is the relation of the particular to the general, that is, human nature, in such a way that the particular is still in view. This is unlike science where there is no particular. My claim is that political theory is reductive in character in that some feature of human conduct is affirmed as necessarily central to human life such that all the practices constitutive of social life are not seen as autonomous, but as functionally related to and dependent upon this central concern. A knowledge of the natures of these various practices is to be determined by reference to what is asserted of human nature as such. A cursory glance at the history of political thought, employing the political theory model, reveals the diversity of the allegedly central features and I need only list a few here – to live on this earth while at the same time being within the heavenly city; to appeal to the principle whereby we should and must pursue pleasure and avoid pain in all activity; to recognise that it is in acting in compliance with the law that we are truly free.

A further illustration of my point of view can be given by an example from the work of Herbert Spencer[5] who holds the view that political and social life should be understood in terms of a theory of evolution, yet goes on to make recommendations concerning political and social practice. If the notion 'evolution' were construed in a scientific sense then we could not introduce the idea of recommendation. It is done so illicitly in Spencer by his understanding human nature as an independently identifiable entity. In the context of an explanatory structure a predictive assertion such as 'it will be the case that P' is justified by reference to our knowledge of sequential change. However, if we were to say that 'it ought to be the case that P' then we seek a justification for a recommendation which, to be supplied theoretically, must indicate something independent of what an explanation of P coming about would consist of. This is what I argue we cannot have.

Someone may object here that the difference in structure between natural science and political theory does not show political theory to be incoherent. To meet this objection my argument must take a more straightforwardly epistemological turn. In order to establish theoretical knowledge, that is, in the case of political theory, knowledge of a general kind which would feature in an explanatory account, we must have some means or procedure for the establishment of a claim to knowledge as acceptable on objective grounds; we would require, in short, some procedure of verification or falsification. In the case of political theory this is what we lack – we have nothing analogous to experimentation in natural science, or the appeal to evidence in history. What we do have are more or less elaborate conceptual schemes which posit a reference to some reality, but do not provide us with, or occur in the context of, a means by which we may make a reference to this reality outside the conceptual scheme in question. This is not to say that these schemes are meaningless, but that they do not give us knowledge because they are not testable. It will be my concern at the end of this chapter to suggest wherein the sense of these 'schemes' may be thought to lie. However, for the moment I wish to return to the discussion of political theory.

In case it still be thought that my remarks pertain only to a misuse of the vocabulary of natural science by certain political theorists, and thus are not general in import, let me give, in addition, an example from a writer who does not employ the language of natural science at all. Martin Luther, in his 'tract' 'Secular authority: to what extent it should be obeyed',[6] argues, on theological grounds, that the relationship that a man can have to God is guaranteed by Him and is logically independent of how things go in the world. However, he then proceeds to argue that the secular authorities should not attempt to interfere in this relationship. Now this is logically inconsistent on the trivial point that 'should' implies 'can'. My claim here is that in order to make his point stand Luther would have to bring in some other specification of what it is to have a relation to God which is extra-theological and that this would end up as an appeal to what we know of human nature. Only then do we have the theoretically determined reason for saying that secular authorities should not attempt to act in the realm of faith. Thus we are confronted by the same point again: we have an a-temporally grounded statement of what is, and a recommendatory statement; in order to remove the logical contradiction involved in presenting them as interdependent some extra knowledge must be elicited of human nature.

Let me now summarise what I take to be the implications of what I have said so far.

(1) We are faced with the impossibility of understanding the term 'human nature' as having reference within a political association which could supply any person with knowledge relevant to the formation of an intention to act politically.

(2) The conclusion from this is that political and social life cannot be accounted for in any exercise that falls within the confines of the political theory model. And as the aim of political theory is to explain and to be relevant to the practice of politics the exercise is incoherent.

To further elucidate this account I should like to introduce the notion of epiphenomenalism which, I think, is a central characteristic of political theory. K. R. Minogue, in an article entitled 'Epiphenomenalism in politics: the quest for political reality',[7] presents this notion very clearly and I think I can best make my point by brief reference to this piece. In his article Minogue argues that political activity is not the kind of subject that can be objectively understood by viewing it in the context of a theoretical explanatory structure. To make his point Minogue produces what is, in effect, an anti-reductionist case: 'Epiphenomenalism in politics is the doctrine that political events are epiphenomena determined necessarily according to the laws of some explanatory structure external to politics.'[8] What springs to mind most readily here is the way in which some Marxists have proffered an understanding of political activity which is heavily deterministic. However, I do not wish to pursue this line of inquiry which would be one of the methodological concern to the would-be political theorist. The point I wish to make is that epiphenomenalism is a logical characteristic of political theory *per se*. The difference between the purely logical and methodological concerns is to be found in how an anti-reductionist argument is formulated and how it is applied. I wish to claim that talking in terms of deterministic laws is but one form of reductionism in the examination of politics and that reductionism is a formal or logical feature of the very nature of political theory; the particular forms that reductionism takes is a contingent matter *vis-à-vis* my interest here. In short, then, I see epiphenomenalism as a formal characteristic of political theory, because that exercise consists of the attempt to understand politics in terms of something else, something other than it is. I say this because I want to make it clear that my remarks do not have the substance of possible methodological objections to particular engagements in political theory, but are intended to pertain to the nature of our interpretation of statements made within the realm of what is, and has been, termed political theory. And I want to claim that a certain conception of what our understanding consists of is incoherent and that therefore we should attempt to formulate a different philosophical conception of what contribution these statements could make to our understanding.

The consequences of taking epiphenomenalism as a central feature of political theory is that it entails a focus of interest such that our specification of what ideology consists of, and its relation to political theory, will not be given in terms of methodological objections that it is possible to make against any one contribution to political theory, which is something of the kind of argument Marx used to distinguish what he termed 'ideology' from 'science'. It will be given in terms of an indication of the misconception we have of a particular language use, that is, of what contribution such a use of language can make to our understanding, and that misconception is, quite simply, political theory. Let me make this clear by clarifying my distinction between the nature of a form of inquiry and questions of methodology. What I have in mind here is that when a methodological objection is brought to a method of investigation (e.g. Marxist analysis of social and economic structures), it is not the enterprise itself which is brought into question, but a particular method employed in it. That is to say, we assume what I term a 'propositional context' when we bring methodological objections to some contribution. However, the scepticism I have adduced here is not methodological in character. It is not concerned with the correct or incorrect grounding of any one claim made in political theory, but is general in nature: it is the thesis that to conceive of the concept 'political theory' as denoting a particular language-use is a mistake and a mistake for the reason that no such theoretical investigation is possible.

In order to reiterate the point that the objection to political theory is general and not methodological in nature, that is, that it is not an objection to various methods of establishing theoretical knowledge about man, but to the very idea of human nature as an object of inquiry, we can turn to the political thought of John Locke. Here the relation between theory and practice is not given in an analogous way to the relation of scientific knowledge to technology, but in terms of a metaphysical delineation of man's identity by recourse to laws of nature which are apprehendable by 'Reason'. In so far as this is an appeal to 'Reason' these 'laws' map out the pre-political, or apolitical, relation between men in a normative way. Civil government, if it is to be legitimate, institutionalises these relations, as set out by the laws of nature, in an authoritative structure. The laws of nature then, provide us with a set of criteria for the determination of just arrangements, but they do so only in so far as they tell us about the nature of man. Now it may at first seem curious to say that the laws of nature of which Locke speaks purport to tell us about the nature of man, because, surely, *qua* laws, they are regulative of man's conduct? I think this is to understand them too much by analogy with laws which are straightforwardly the outcome of legal enactment within any one state. The 'just' arrangements which Locke's laws of nature speak of are 'just' in virtue of God's ordained purpose for the life of man. By 'Reason' we apprehend God's will in the laws of nature. Man's identity is then, I claim, given in terms of a purpose ordained by God. Anyone who apprehends the laws of nature, by 'Reason', has then, of necessity, apprehended his purpose as ordained by God. He has apprehended his identity as agent, and in Locke's case he has apprehended it in terms of a religiously specified end, that is, salvation. Now we do not ordinarily talk of laws as conferring upon us an identity in conduct in any sense but a legal identity, that is one specified in the system of law itself.

And I think there is good reason to hold that to speak in this extraordinary fashion is incoherent. It is incoherent because we have to be in the position whereby we can speak of the regulative aspect of law as not having significance in a positive, that is, politically determined legal system, but in terms of law mirroring, or being a reflection or particular manifestation of, our identity as defined by reference to some logically independent knowledge.[9] The history of political theory is the history of the attempt to delineate the means by which we may specify that identity. The methods that have been employed in order to specify that identity have varied in conceptual character, but their end has been the same: to state in some theoretical fashion, the identity of man, that is, human nature, and then to relate that to actual legally defined associations we call states, with the result that we have criteria for the rightness or wrongness of our practices and activities.

At the beginning of this chapter I stated that I held the view that the terms 'political theory' and 'political ideology' were not synonyms, and perhaps I can now introduce the concept 'ideology' by saying why it is that I do not think we are justified so far in holding their meanings to be equivalent. The term 'political theory' was introduced in order that an investigation could proceed to determine the nature of a particular language-use, that is, what I have termed a propositional context. This is not an empirical, but a conceptual question. Thus if anybody understands my use of the term 'political theory' he will understand an account of the nature of a certain kind of theorising about political association. The purpose of my argument has been to justify a sceptical position, which is that no coherent account can be given of the theoretical exercise constituting political theory. My point now is: so much the worse for this particular attempt to represent the logical nature of a particular language-use. Whatever is effected in it, so long as the object of understanding is still unspecified, is not the generation of theoretical knowledge. What we have ruled out, by advancing arguments against political theory as a form of inquiry, is, as it were, a possibility. The term 'political theory' has no reference because we cannot attribute any coherent meaning to it. However, if we introduce the term 'political ideology' into our investigation we may be better off: better off because this concept does not, necessarily, imply the particular relation between theory and practice which proved to be the main difficulty for the political theory model. Let me give an example here to indicate what I have in mind.

As we all know, the first sentence of the first chapter of *The Communist Manifesto* reads: 'The history of all hitherto existing society is the history of class struggles.' I shall call this sentence S. Now if we want to know what contribution in principle S can make to our understanding we will have to have a knowledge, more or less explicit, of the propositional context in which it can be adduced as a meaningful sentence. The political theory model attempts to provide such a context. If we were to place the sentence S within this context then I think we would have an analysis looking something like this:

> The sentence S expresses the proposition that the history of all hitherto existing society is the history of class struggles.
> This proposition is either true or false.
> The epistemological justification for the assertion of the proposition, is to be located in Marx's theory of human nature where 'alienation' is the concept that specifies the nature of the relations between men, nature and production.

The political theory model, then, supplies us with an understanding of how the terms 'true' and 'false' will be utilised; it gives us a pre-presentation of their possible employment. However, if, as I have argued, political theory is incoherent then we can have no uses for the concepts 'true' and 'false', which are dependent upon a certain sense being made. If we do come to this conclusion, then are we not forced to say of the original sentence S that it is nonsensical? By this I mean that the sentence is meaningless in that it does not express a proposition which can be judged as true or as false. Well, at one level to say of the sentence S that it is nonsensical is perfectly in order, but it presupposes that we are working with the thesis that political theory is incoherent. In other words I propose this formulation: the assertion 'the sentence S is nonsensical' is true or false if, and only if, that sentence is located in the propositional context we call political theory and is true if, and only if, that context is incoherent. Thus the use of the concept 'nonsense' presupposes an attack upon the employment of a propositional context, just as the concepts 'true' and 'false' presuppose the existence of such a context for their use. In other words questions of truth and falsity, or, more broadly, questions concerning themselves with the justification or criticism of the grounds for an assertion which is to be judged true or false, are internally related to a propositional context, and cannot, in themselves, bring that context into question. However, a judgement concerning nonsense is one which entails a relation, on the part of the person making the judgement, to the more or less explicit knowledge an utterer has of the structure of the proposition in question. Thus such a judgement relates to the semantic intention of the utterer, that is, to what kind of contribution he wishes to make to our understanding. A judgement of nonsensicality entails, for its truth, the incoherence of the conception which, in principle, allows the intention. The incoherence in this particular instance is the relation between theory and practice entailed in the political theory model.

The notion 'political ideology' is not synonymous with the notion 'political theory' just in so far as we can give under its name a representation of a form of thinking different in nature from the political theory model. Just in so far as it is different then the application of the term 'nonsense' cannot be made in this context in the way that it could be if we assumed the political theory model. The difference between political theory and political ideology is conceptual in nature, and this is just what we are investigating, the conceptual characteristics of a particular use of language. The particular conceptual difference I have in mind is, I think, well illustrated by Rush Rhees:

> If a man is determined to fight for liberty (for the furtherance of liberty in this society) – then fine. But if he says he is determined to fight for liberty *for the reason* that – . . . then I lose interest, and similarly if he is determined to fight for the achievement of communism.[10]

What he is indicating to us is the confusion that may arise, in philosophy, if we conflate the ethical with the investigatory. (This is, as it were, analogous to the confusion which occurs in our philosophical understanding of mathematics, according to Wittgenstein, if we interpret mathematics as investigation into some aspect of reality, in the Platonic sense; if this confusion, if it be one, does occur then it is so much the worse for our philosophical understanding, not for mathematics itself.) What we must do then if we are to employ the notion 'political ideology' is disregard, for the purposes of starting the investigation, the political theory model, and this means that we shall not employ the idea of 'investigation': this notion became redundant in our inquiry once we had rejected political theory as being a coherent propositional context.

Someone might object at this point that it is far from clear that the argument adduced is adequate for the conclusion I have set out. They may say that even if we adopt an attitude of scepticism towards the exercise we have called political theory, we may still say that one of the central characteristics of ideological thinking is the conflation of the ethical and the investigatory. People who have thought ideologically are people who have made, however implicitly, this confusion. After saying this we then specify what the use of ideological language can effect, and say that this is in opposition to what the person who thinks, *not* necessarily speaks, ideologically actually holds it does effect. So even in this account of ideology we do specify something apart from the incoherence of political theory, but nevertheless the latter notion is still of great importance.

There is, I think, a telling objection to this thesis and it is that it involves the conflation of an account we might give of how it comes about that any one person, or group of persons, actually employs language in an ideological fashion – in which case the notion 'ideology' must be already specified, or at least bracketed, because this is plainly an empirical matter – with a description of what that language use consists of, that is, what any user of language can, in principle, effect when he uses language in this way, which is a conceptual not an empirical matter concerning explanations applying to actual people. Talk within the empirical category is, perhaps, well illustrated by Minogue when he states that: 'It is understandable . . . that amongst audiences with a taste for science or philosophy political justification will begin to take on the same form as academic disciplines.'[11] My point can be reinforced by our noting the asymmetric relation of dependence between a theory of ideology and an explanatory empirical investigation. Obviously an exercise of the latter kind will be responsive to a theory of ideology, but we cannot work this procedure in reverse because all such an empirical investigation will provide us with is a stipulative definition in terms of the delineation of a subject matter. Such a procedure is, of course, question-begging if our interest is philosophical. A philosopher is concerned with the notion 'ideology' because straightforward definitions do not give him a satisfactory grasp on the meaning of the term; he has to proceed in such a way that he may locate the meaning in an examination of a complex practice, or group of related practices. (This is obviously the task of political philosophy as a whole.) As such the meaning of the term will emerge from the coherent formulation of the nature of those practices. What is philosophically problematic about any one concept, or rather a hint at how it is that concepts can be philosophically difficult, is probably given by saying that, in the utterance of certain assertions we feel that the retort 'it all depends what you mean by . . .' is justified, while in our ordinary use of language such a reply would be unjust.

According to the argument of this chapter we cannot conceive of political theory as a use of language which creates theoretical knowledge relevant to political practice. One entailment from the preceding argument is that it is peculiarly one-sided to conceive of ideology only in the context of an ill-formed attempt at investigation, and then hold the view that questions of meaning are redundant. What has been ruled out is a possibility, but what we must be careful to note is that the possibility arose in philosophy, that is, we are following the general point that questions of possibility arise within a form of reasoning. For example, the impossibility of squaring the circle is given in mathematics by the proof that *pi* is transcendental; if we generalise this point we see that questions of possibility arise within forms of understanding; they are not determined in abstraction from them. The concept political theory, or rather the analysis of the concept's meaning, does not yield a description of a coherent language-use. This is of consequence in political philosophy, and one consequence is that we cannot, without further investigation, use the political theory model to give a representation of what the ideological use of language consists of. To say this is not to assert that empirical work employing the concept 'ideology' cannot proceed utilising the political theory model, with or without scepticism towards what the model represents, but that we cannot expect much progress in this field until we have the theory of ideology properly delineated, because without this we cannot not be agreed on what we are talking about. What proposals, then, can be given concerning the substance of the theory of ideology? To conclude I will discuss some of the notions which I think can usefully contribute to the construction of such a theory.

So far it may be thought that any contribution I have made to the theory of ideology is primarily negative, but this view needs some qualification. What I have tried to do is, first, argue, without recourse to the notion of ideology, that a certain conception of the relation between theory and practice is a misconception and, secondly, I have sought to suggest that the attempt to apprehend the sense of ideological thinking in this area is mistaken. In order to support this suggestion I should now like to outline, in abstract, what I think a positive account would consist of and to do this I want to contrast two senses of the term 'belief'. In this way I wish to show how ideological statements are related to practice in terms of agents' ethical dispositions, as against the incoherence involved in thinking that they are related to experience in terms of a prescriptive theory. To begin, then, I will briefly outline the two senses of the term 'belief' that I have in mind.

First, there is the case of beliefs that consist of propositions assented to which can have some form of epistemological justification, that is, it can be said of such beliefs that they are well, or ill-founded, by appeal to some evidential basis. Within this class of beliefs we can place those beliefs of which we say that they are either true or false. Secondly, we have a class of beliefs which do not admit of questions concerning their truth or falsity, or of their being well grounded in some evidential basis. These beliefs concern the way in which we judge or evaluate objects or actions in terms of their ethical, religious or aesthetic characters. That is, they are constitutive of the standards we employ in such evaluations.

Beliefs of the second kind are neither true nor false in the sense that they do not contain a proposition saying *how things are*, but involve the recommendation *how things ought to be*, on non-instrumental grounds. Another way of putting this would be to say that they are normative not factual. Thus, in short, and crudely put, we assign truth-values to propositions by checking how things are, while in the case of religious and ethical judgements we test experience by reference to our beliefs and assign the values 'right' and 'wrong' to conduct itself.

Now it is, of course, notorious that the major theme of some moral philosophy has been the concern to give an account of the logical nature of such beliefs, and one question that has arisen in this context is 'how can we be justified in thinking that our beliefs are the right ones?'. The correct response to this question is, I believe, that we cannot be if the justification sought is thought to have a direct connection with knowledge, that is, that which is testable. The point here is, I think, put well by Wittgenstein in his conversation with Waismann:

> Schlick says that theological ethics contains two conceptions of the essence of the Good. According to the more superficial interpretation, the Good is good because God wills it; according to the deeper interpretation, God wills the Good because it is good. I think that the first conception is the deeper one: Good is what God orders. For this cuts off the path to any and every explanation 'why' it is good, while the second conception is precisely the superficial, rationalistic one, which proceeds as if what is good could still be given some foundation.[12]

What we should do, then, if the suggestion here is accepted, is reject the epistemological question concerning justification, and formulate our inquiry around questions such as 'how are we able to come to have beliefs of this kind?' and 'how are these beliefs related to our actions and practices?'.

It is here that the theory of ideology can make a contribution to ethics, and it can do so by focusing on ideology as being the language of adherence. By this I mean that ideological thinking should be considered as the elaboration of a language rendering experience intelligible in the light of, or by reference to, some picture or conception of men as socially related beings. I use the term 'picture' and 'conception' because they relate ideology to ethics and not to notions such as 'theory' and 'knowledge'. Pictures or conceptions, unlike theories or other kinds of claim to knowledge, are not testable; they are what we use to judge experience by.

At the same time these conceptions are the kind of things that we have to adhere to in some way. This is where ideological thinking comes in and is to be understood in terms of the notion of an ideal.

An ideal, sincerely believed in, is an idea of how persons both *can* and *should* live. Here we have the introduction of two modal terms, 'can' and 'should', where the former relates to a possibility to be accounted for in some way, and the latter involves the elaboration of an ethical recommendation. Now what I want to claim is that we are introduced to ideals, as things that can be believed in, by a picture or conception of man, presented in general terms, which fills out the possibility involved and elaborates, or presents, to us, the ethical 'should' in some appealing fashion. This is what I mean by calling ideology the language of adherence.

The notions 'can' and 'should' are also related in another connected way: to fill out a possibility as being real, and a 'should' as being an ethical recommendation it is incumbent upon us to take up, an account must be proffered of how an ideological picture is related to the temporal here and now. The ideologist must, as it were, locate *us* in his picture presenting how things are and should be. We must, then, appear in the ideologist's conception as existing individuals who can act either appropriately or inappropriately. The questions in the theory of ideology on this account become centred on two themes: first, how ideological beliefs are related to activity and, secondly, how ideological beliefs can be formulated and presented to us. However, having rejected the implied relation of theory to practice found in political theory, the form of the discussion will be that primarily of ethics, and perhaps something analogous to aesthetics, and not an epistemological concern with explanation and prescriptive theory.

NOTES: CHAPTER 4

1 J. Plamenatz, *Ideology* (Macmillan, London, 1971).
2 What I say here forms part of a much larger and more complex debate concerning methodology in relation to what is termed 'the history of political thought'. This is a debate outside the compass of this paper.
3 This is stated explicitly by R. M. MacIver in his book *The Modern State* (Clarendon Press, Oxford, 1926), p. 3: 'The whole of this volume is devoted to answering the question, What *is* the state?' (emphasis in original).
4 M. Mandelbaum, 'The problem of covering laws', in P. Gardiner (ed.), *The Philosophy of History* (Oxford University Press, London, 1974).
5 H. Spencer, 'The social organism', in D. Macrae (ed.), *Herbert Spencer, 'The Man Versus the State'* (Pelican, Harmondsworth, 1969).
6 M. Luther, 'Secular authority: to what extent it should be obeyed', in J. Dillenberger (ed.), *Martin Luther, Selections from his Writings*, (Doubleday-Anchor, New York, 1961).
7 K. R. Minogue, 'Epiphenomenalism in politics: the quest for political reality', *Political Studies*, vol. xx, no. 4, December 1972, pp. 462–74.

8 ibid., p. 469.
9 Hegel holds the view that law, as an aspect or level of 'Right', identifies the will in terms of what is rational and what is irrational in its exercise. The system of 'Objective Mind' gives us, thereby, a specification of our identity as social agents.
10 Rush Rhees, *Without Answers* (Routledge & Kegan Paul, London, 1969), pp. 84–5 (emphasis in original).
11 K. R. Minogue, op. cit., p. 470.
12 L. Wittgenstein, in F. Waismann, 'Notes on Talks with Wittgenstein', trans. M. Black, in *The Philosophical Review*', vol. LXXIV, 1965, p. 15.

5
The Place of Ideology in Political Life

One well-known inquiry into the relationship between theory and practice is designed to question the belief that the political achievement of an adherent of an ideology is largely the result of his having mastered the relationship between a set of principles and the pursuit of political objectives. Michael Oakeshott's famous critique has obvious implications for any evaluation of the status of technical instruction in the practice of politics.[1] If it can be shown that there are principles to be mastered in political education then we may expect the diligent apprentice of Mill or Marx to be a more capable reformer or revolutionary than those less inclined, or able, to pursue the intricacies of utilitarianism or dialectical materialism. If it cannot be shown that principles have this value then it will be difficult to maintain that political education has a technical character comparable with, say, that to be found in laboratory training. The fact that the successful scientist displays that he knows more than the principles of scientific investigation when he carries out an experiment does not prejudice the claim that he could not conduct it without first having acquired technical knowledge of the kind that enables him to conceive of his observations as evidence for or against a hypothesis concerning a physical process.

It is not clear that a knowledge of political principles is equally indispensable in the case of political conduct. The claim that political conduct is the art of applying political principles is questionable. It portrays what Oakeshott calls 'rationalism in politics'. Even when presented in conjunction with detailed prescriptions of the kind we find in Mill's *Representative Government*, political principles either remain rooted in the realm of conceptual understanding appropriate to reaching conclusions about the distinctive character of political activity (rather than transplant to that appropriate to reaching political decisions), or their intelligibility is parasitic upon the practical understanding displayed by those who are masters of the art of politics in a particular culture. Political theories present to us an understanding brought to, rather than an understanding creative in, political life.

Their intelligent interpretation depends more upon our possessing a knowledge of how logically we can deploy the vocabulary of politics, or on our having served an apprenticeship in a political practice, than an intelligent intervention in politics depends upon a command of their literature. At best they contribute to an analysis of political understanding, or an 'abridgement' of political experience – a representation, or caricature, of these features meaningful only to those who know the face. Political principles cannot be applied to guide our political activity in the way that the activity of those who have mastered the practice is informed by their experience of its changing procedures and circumstances. Consequently, as the focus of education in the practice of politics, it must be judged defective. Oakeshott concludes therefore that reliance upon it is dangerously misleading.

Another well-known inquiry into the relationship between the intellectual achievement of the ideologist and the political performance of those who adhere to his conclusions is concerned to query the possibility of there being a genuine theoretical understanding of the process of economic and social evolution of use to those who would engineer political change. Karl Popper's investigation is obviously also supposed to be one of practical importance:[2] if it is the case that either Mill or Marx has determined the conditions for desirable social evolution, then those who are aware of them may well succeed in their endeavour to create a planned society simply from knowing what can, and cannot, be accomplished in the world. If not, and they are misled, then their efforts are likely to prove to be in vain. The question is: is their confidence well-founded or are they mistaken? Again the answer depends upon whether or not political education is technical. In this case the emphasis is placed on the availability of technical information concerning opportunities that we may take, rather than on the principle we should apply, to achieve the organisation of public affairs in the best possible way. Popper's conclusion is that there is no such information available. Theories of social, economic and political development of the kind we find in the works of Mill and Marx, particularly Marx, are not, properly speaking, scientific. They are not capable of falsification by reference to empirical observation. In a different, but comparable, way to Oakeshott, Popper finds the weakness of ideological argument to be a failure directly to refer to, and give information about, the world. He too is sceptical of the claim that they offer appropriate instruction independent of that which we acquire in the course of a political career, and, hence he regards it as dangerous to believe that they give grounds for confidence in undertaking political innovation.

This chapter is not intended to pursue directly either of the above lines of inquiry in the form that Oakeshott and Popper have presented them, although it will, at various points, touch upon matters which lie in their path. It is an investigation into a related, but different, aspect of the relationship between ideology and political action. It is not concerned to challenge the thesis that, in preparing a man for a political career it is a mistake to claim that ideological works perform the role, for example, of either laboratory manuals in training a scientist, or textbooks on meteorology in training a weather forecaster. It will try to locate the particular incoherence involved in such a thesis. However, in doing so, it is intended to show that the admission of a mistake of this kind cannot preclude the claim that ideology offers an equivalent form of instruction in the practice of politics. It may appear to be an impossible mongrel resulting from the confusion of the theoretical with the practical mode of discourse, but it survives because there is something which can be done with it and done well. It will be argued that it offers something like the vocabulary and grammar of the language of party political relationships without a command of which we cannot hope to succeed in modern political life. Ideological education, it will be claimed, has an essential part to play in modern politics in spite of the fact that many of the claims which have been made for its capacity to carry information to the political participant are subject to philosophical objection.

It is not altogether clear whether, prior to the work of Oakeshott and Popper, there was a danger of the politically innocent being misled by the sophistry of ideologists. Today, however, they are more likely to be misled by the sophistication of these philosophers. The very strength of the anti-rationalist and anti-holist cases is such that their destruction of what may be taken to be the substance of the ideologist's claims has obscured the fact that the student of an ideology does, without putting his political ambitions at risk, derive instruction from its literature. There remains a question to be answered about the relationship between ideology and action, after the claim that ideological education instructs us in the pursuit of political achievement has been dismissed. If it is the case that the rationalist is mistaken in believing that the relationship between political theory and practice is a potent one, except in so far as this belief encourages a misplaced confidence in his capacity to improve the world, then what is the force of the statement that the 'rationalist is a dangerous and expensive character to have in control of affairs . . .'?[3] How, we might ask, in the case of politics, can so deluded a man ever get into a position of control of the affairs of a nation? Given that the careers of Robespierre, Lenin and Hitler did not culminate in the creation of the promised new order, and that their ultimate failure is one that may be attributed to their rationalism, the question still remains, how did they manage to gain the power necessary to promote such spectacular disasters? If 'the alleged analogy between physical engineering and holistic social engineering breaks down . . . since the scientific basis of its plans is simply nowhere',[4] how is it that 'holistic control, which must lead to the equalization not of human rights but of human minds, would mean the end of progress'?[5] If it is possible that a mistaken claim about the world can lead to the end of progress, presumably the ideology that advances it, through those who accept it, must have a decisive influence on the course of events. The question is: how? Popper, like Oakeshott, believes the modern to be an ideological age, but neither has explained why the ideologically committed have succeeded in dominating our lives, rather than finding their projects resulting in early and abject failure – an experience from which they might be expected to learn the obvious lesson. It is to this question that the following reflections are intended to be considered as an answer.

Let us begin by examining independently the claim that it is a mistake to believe that a knowledge of opportunities to improve the world, and instruction in the business of exploiting them, is readily available to those who pursue masterpieces of 'political theory'. According to Popper and Oakeshott, 'political theories' do not provide a specification of what has to be done, and how it has to be done, to succeed in politics. This implies that there is not, on the face of it, a Marxist opportunity for, and way of, overthrowing a government, any more than there is a Marxist occasion for, or way of, taking a bath, or a liberal opportunity for, or way of, changing a law, any more than there is a liberal occasion for, or way of, reading a book. Ideologies do not indicate the direction we should take, or methods we should adopt, to achieve what we claim to be our ideological goals. There is no obvious sense to be made of talk about putting a 'political theory' into practice. The history of the Soviet Union, for example, does not serve as a guide to the ideology called Marxism; neither do the doctrines of Marx and Lenin serve as a guide to Soviet history. In addition it will not do to suggest that this is the result of the Soviet Communist Party having failed to live up to its ideals, or its leaders having failed to master the 'principles' of revolutionary government. Marxism is not a 'theory' that could have been put into practice in Russia had the Soviet Communist Party acted more like a party of 'communists' unless the ideological commitment of the members of a party can determine what they should do, and how, and it is clear that to be told that a 'communist' society is one in which each contributes according to his ability and takes according to his need affords us no description of the kind of arrangements a 'communist' society will have, and how they are to be established; hence, we cannot calculate from it which decisions are to be regarded as correctly taken to create 'communism' and which do not. The definition tells us no more about socialist conduct here and now than the statement that all history is the history of class struggle tells us anything about what happened in the past. Although many have not in fact been counted, any political action could, in Marxist terms, count as a step towards the creation of a 'communist' society, just as any political action can be seen as a manifestation of 'class struggle'. It was not difficult for Stalin, as the official ideologist of the Soviet Communist Party, to justify the purging of old Bolsheviks from its ranks, or the Soviet Union forming an alliance with Nazi Germany. And it is not just a case of some ideological formulations failing to serve as a guide to political action because they are too vague. They are all necessarily incapable of being specific. We should not be surprised that the opposition to a political movement cannot, on the basis of a knowledge of its ideology, determine what politics its adherents are obliged to support, in the way that we can, by consulting the statute book, determine which actions those who have certain legal obligations will be justified in condemning. Ideological talk, unlike legal talk, does not give us information about the world in which we live. It cannot carry the appropriate descriptive content. The killing of a man described in a court as happening in a particular way may be judged to be a case of justifiable homicide, or murder, in what might appear to be the same way as a violent seizure of political power may be acclaimed by a Marxist to be a 'revolution' or dismissed as a mere *coup d'état*, but there is an essential difference.

The judgement of a court that an action constituted the crime of murder gives us to understand that this killing, unlike some others, cannot adequately be described without it being stated that it was committed with malicious intent. There has to be a difference in the accurate description of the action judged by a court to be murder and that judged to be justifiable homicide but there does not have to be a difference between the correct description of the event the Marxist claims to be a 'revolution' and that which he claims to be a *coup d'état* or 'counter-revolution'. It may be said that for the Marxist the difference between the two actions is that the former is committed by a Marxist and the latter by a liberal or nazi, and this distinction is not one made between the actions as such. Clearly, it would not do for a judge to find a man guilty of murder on grounds of his ideological opinions. In calling an example of the crime treason a 'revolution', a Marxist does not succeed in distinguishing it from any other illegal seizure of power, beyond the fact that he, and those who claim to share his convictions, approve of its occurrence. His instructing his followers to start a 'revolution' cannot in itself tell them anything more than that he desires that they effect a change in the world. No particular order of the kind 'kill Mr X' has been given. There is no point in our scrutinising the evidence for the success of any attempted compliance with the instruction to start a 'revolution' with a view to discovering whether the event really is 'revolution', and not a *coup d'état,* in the way that we might review the evidence presented to a court to determine whether or not its judgement that a killing is murder, and not justifiable homicide, is well founded. For a court to decide that the killing of a man is murder involves the application of a technical term in law. If this were not the case it would not be possible for a court of appeal to overrule the decisions of a lower court on the grounds that it was not in accordance with the law. In order that a man be able to exercise his authority to pass legal judgements the law must clearly distinguish between classes of actions, and this is not the case with an ideology. The official ideologist of a group or party cannot command respect for his ideological statements by demonstrating that they refer to, and are borne out by, the relevant facts. He can only refer to the doctrine in which they make ideological sense. In a court a revolution, if the term is used at all, is an illegal seizure of power, just as a communist is a man who is a member of a communist party. In Marxist terminology a 'communist' seizure of power is a 'revolution', just as a 'communist' is, if not an 'unalienated' man, at least not a victim of 'false consciousness'. To substantiate an ideological claim we must refer to the doctrine to which it belongs. It is its sense that has to be shown. To substantiate a claim about a matter of fact we must refer to the world. It is its truth that is at stake. Lenin may relate the ideological term 'revolution' to the event known as the Russian Revolution, but he cannot refer to that event with this term without promoting ideological controversy. The relationship between the ideological term 'revolution' and the name 'the Russian Revolution' is one of historical contingency, not convention. Ideological terms like 'revolution', if technical terms, are not technical terms like 'murder'. They are incapable of specifying a class of actions.

The argument against the claim that ideologies embody genuine scientific hypotheses about the process of economic and political development takes a similar form to that against the claim that they provide the distinctions between classes of actions required in their description. It is, that just as terms like 'revolution' are of a different kind from terms like murder, terms like 'dialectic' are different in kind from terms like 'condensation.' Ideologies do not refer to processes a knowledge of which can indicate how the world will change. They do not possess the appropriate conceptual framework to carry the kind of information we derive from experimental observations. They recommend changes in our conception of human relationships which, it is claimed, will influence the decisions of men. These are not the same kind of changes that follow a change in physical relationships. Any change in human behaviour that may follow a change in our conception of human relationships cannot register on an instrument in a manner specified in terms of a scientific law. For example, the fact that men in the market are now acting in a way that will help them make a profit, or that the candidates of one party are now acting in a way that will lead to their succeeding at the polls, is not something that we can measure. It is something that we assess. It is what the account books and opinion polls suggest. Economic and political forecasts are of a different kind from, for example, weather forecasts. They are not based upon the causal relationship between such measurable factors as changes in temperature and humidity. Economic booms and slumps and electoral swings are not like droughts and monsoons. We cannot expect changes in real income, or changes of government, in the same way that we may expect and, more important, induce, the fall of rain. The reliability of both weather forecasts and economic and political forecasts depends upon up-to-date information gathered in the appropriate field, but where the former involves knowing the effect of a physical interaction the latter involves speculation as to changes of opinion and the result of human decisions. It is logically impossible to generate genuine scientific theories about economic and political development. However, it does not follow that those who have claimed that their ideology offers a guide to political action, both in terms of the rules to be followed in pursuing ideal relationships, and in predicting the outcome of steps taken to realise them, have disastrously misled their adherents. They cannot substantiate their claim to possess technical knowledge of the kind to be found in laboratory manuals or textbooks on meteorology, but the fact that their ideological talk cannot communicate these kinds of technical information entails the fact that it cannot communicate misinformation of these kinds too. Politicians may not derive the kind of technical superiority over the layman possessed by the experimental or applied scientist from being ideologically committed, but they are certainly not led to act on misinformation by the belief that their ideology has provided information. Moreover, the possibility remains that they derive a different kind of advantage from their commitment from that of possessing the kinds of technical information discussed.

No matter what the adherent of an ideology believes, he cannot be engaged in achieving objectives prescribed by a knowledge of the arrangements of an ideal society pursued in the light of a theory of social evolution. When the Marxist tells us that he is engaged in the 'revolutionary' struggle to bring about 'communism', he indicates to those who share his conviction that he expects them to give him some practical assistance. He has not described his strategy and tactics. He has not stated his intention in terms of the concrete steps he proposes to take, or the reasons why he believes that they are efficacious. But he has indicated, that, in his judgement, what he is doing is what Marxists should be doing in the world. Although there is no identifiable course of action which only Marxists should follow, only a Marxist can, without practising a deception, *join* other Marxists in doing what they happen to have decided is the best thing to do. There is no reason to believe that ideological talk, because of its epistemological incoherence, gets in the way of common sense and hinders the adherent in the assessment of projects and situations, and there is every reason to believe that an adherent's command of the vocabulary of his ideology does enable him to communicate an identity without which the formation of the peculiar relationship of group or party membership is impossible. Ideological talk may be irrelevant to predicting political developments and making policy decisions, but it is not irrelevant to communicating commitment.

It is true that Marxism cannot assist the historian in writing Soviet history, but it is equally true that the historian of the Soviet Union cannot locate the ideological significance that the events of 1917 had for the Bolsheviks, and have for those who support the party they founded. A historical account of the actions which brought about the fall of the tsarist regime does not suggest that, in 1917, the world witnessed the foundation of the 'dictatorship of the proletariat' or the beginning of 'communist' society. The historian cannot make sense with these terms. They are evaluative, not descriptive. The vocabulary of Marxism can only be used properly by a Marxist in the context of political engagement. It cannot be used by the historian, or by the adherent of other ideologies, without confusion or deception, and this is a fact of enormous political importance.

Without the doctrines of Marxism there could have been no Bolshevik Party, and without a command of the Marxist vocabulary Lenin would not have been able to convince its members that he was their authentic leader. The possibility of forming a 'revolutionary' party enabled Lenin, and those sympathetic to his cause, to take a common stand on what could usefully be justified in Marxist terms when considering alternative courses of action to bring them to power in Russia. It was a failure to reach a collective decision of this kind that led to their separation from the Mensheviks. Having, in common-sense terms, agreed upon what had to be done to bring them to power, they could then seek the support of all those who could be brought to share their ideological vision and trust their practical judgement. It is not necessary to claim that Lenin, or anybody else, derived his awareness of political opportunities, or intentions to act, from pursuing the work of Marx to establish that the successful pursuit of the Bolshevik programme depended, in part, upon the fact that the language of Marxism was already part of the Russian tradition of political discourse by 1917.

Now not only is it the case that ideological talk cannot prevent those who habitually use it from employing their political experience and commonsense in making political decision, it can liberate them from religious, moral and legal scruples (as distinct from obligations and duties) when it comes to selecting the means they regard as most expedient for achieving their ends. Ideological talk is not like religious, moral, or legal talk. It does not point to the standards and rules by which we are to judge actions affecting existing relationships between persons. It characterises what are claimed to be ideal relationships between those who cannot wilfully violate them, because they are, for example, 'classless', 'racially pure', or 'imbued by the spirit of their nation'. It provides a picture of virtually indestructible relationships said to be created by a special form of collective action designed to transform the human condition; for example, the acts of 'revolution', 'final solution', or 'liberation'.

The modern ideologist is committed to the idea that the standards of human conduct are related to social, economic and legal relationships, the creation or destruction of which must be regarded as the essence of political achievement. He embraces the proposition that a change in the form of human relationships of the kind he desires involves a change in the standard of human conduct. The transformation from 'feudal' to 'civil' society, regarded as progressive in the work of Mill, Spencer and Green, and the transformation of 'capitalism' to 'communism', regarded as 'revolutionary' in the works of Engels, Marx and Lenin, involve a change in what is to be regarded as the standard of good conduct. The efforts of the ideologically committed are not, as they see it themselves, directed at removing a particular inconvenience such as football hooliganism: they are directed at creating relationships and a condition which cannot give rise to behaviour of this kind. They are concerned with such projects as the creation of 'civil' or 'communist' society and the emergence of 'rational' or 'unalienated' man. Both the recognition of the new standards, and the capacity to perform according to them, are deemed impossible without the successful performance of actions which liberals have chosen to call 'reform' and socialists 'revolution'. Performing these constitutes in itself the preparation of contemporary man for the new era. Consequently we can see the importance of ideological doctrines, which illustrate the application of such terms as 'reform' and 'revolution' to what must otherwise appear as unnecessary innovations to those who have not considered forming groups or parties dedicated to acting in their name. No communication exclusive to an ideologically committed group or party is possible without the vocabulary of an ideology being deployed in relation to events. The value of ideological writing cannot be appreciated by those who do not entertain the prospect of the creation of a new man through what is claimed to be informed action. For example, it is possible for a Christian to claim that his stand in the world is not ideological. It requires no ideological commitment, because, as he sees it, the circumstances of the Creation preclude the abolition of evil by human agency. We do not, in this view, have reason to entertain the prospect of a permanent increase in our resistance to sin or the diminishing of temptation through a change in temporal circumstances. It is doubtless possible to deny that a man can reasonably claim to be a Christian who does not accept the Christian view of what constitutes good and evil in the world, but it is not possible to deny that a man is a Christian because he claims the kingdom of God is not of this world. This kind of Christian can claim that the presence of sin in the world cannot be diminished, and that attempts to diminish it are as vain as they are futile. For him there is no more a religious reason for trying to change the order of the Creation than there is scientific reason to try and change the process of nature, or historical reason for attempting to alter the past. This particular Christian has the duty to try to resist sin, but the object of his resistance is not to make the world a different kind of place in which to live. It is the salvation of his soul in the world as he finds it. Moreover, not only can such a Christian sensibly argue that there is nothing he can do to change the nature of the world that will assist others to achieve salvation in it, his own failure to resist the temptation to sin does not deprive him of his Christian identity. He has always the opportunity to repent, and the promise of redemption through prayer. He may not, as a sinner, be entitled to be called a good Christian, but, while he attempts to seek guidance and strength through prayer, it is not possible for us to deny him the name of his faith.

In contrast no such immunity to the loss of a preferred identity can be extended to those who claim to be ideologically committed, but refuse to join with others who share their convictions in an organised attempt to change the world. The man who claims to be a liberal or Marxist, who does not try to transform the world in a way that he believes to be justified by his convictions, cannot be said to be a poor adherent. He cannot be said to be an adherent at all. The man who claims to be a liberal who does not try to support the 'reforming' party, and the man who claims to be a Marxist who refuses to support the 'revolutionary' cause, are guilty of an act of bad faith of the kind we would reprimand in the conduct of those who would have us believe that they are honourable, but do not attempt to honour their promises. Unless we understand that a promise is to be honoured, we do not promise, and the possibility of being honourable in this connection does not exist. Similarly, unless we understand that ideological commitment is logically a commitment to action of political significance, and that this practically requires that we form or join an appropriate group or political party, we do not understand what it is to be an adherent of an ideology. There is no possibility of justifying, on principle, personal quietism or a private campaign in ideological terms.

In certain respects religious and ideological commitments are distinct, but there are others in which they are alike. For example, both have no bearing on the responsibilities of those whose lack of the appropriate conviction places them outside the compass of praise and blame within which adherents evaluate their actions. The standards of performance which govern our religious and political life cannot apply to those who are unable honestly to take part in it. There is no more sense in reproving the atheist for not praying, and the ideologically uncommitted for not joining a group or party, than there is in reproving the Protestant for not attending the Catholic Church, or a conservative for not voting for a socialist party.

At this point there is a useful distinction to be made between the kind of expectation we are entitled to have of the behaviour of men, because they hold certain beliefs, and the kind we are entitled to have of those whose lack of conviction is, in the case in question, an irrelevant consideration. The duty to do what is morally right, or the obligation to comply with the law, for example, is not rooted in a commitment of the kind professed either by the Christian or socialist. They are a duty and an obligation entailed, respectively, in our being human and a member of a political society. Mankind and a political society are distinct from a church and a political party in that they are not voluntary associations of the like-minded. Being human, and being a subject, are not matters of choice. We cannot, for example, choose not to be human by trying to be amoral. Amorality is an imperfection of the kind we attribute to a psychological disorder. It is not an alternative line of conduct open to man. In this respect amorality is distinct from immorality. Thus there is no sense in claiming a right to be a person, or a duty to be a person; we cannot be other than a person, for which reason there is sense in claiming that we have a right to be treated as one, and a duty to treat others in the same way. Similarly, the status of a subject is conferred in law and there is no sense in our talking about a duty to be a subject or a right to be one. We cannot be other than a subject in the modern world, for which reason it is indisputable that we all have legal rights and duties. We cannot alter this status by what we choose to say and we cannot, as a subject, ever claim to be outside the law. (It is true that, in a state, our professing certain convictions may lead to the loss of legal rights, but holding these convictions cannot negate our obligations to comply with the law any more than our not holding them creates the obligation to comply.) In contrast, whether or not we must, to be taken seriously, join a politically ambitious group or party does depend upon the fact that we do, or do not, adhere to the ideology in whose name the group or party claims to act. To be taken seriously the adherent must join it. There is no point to his talk of changing the world if he rejects co-ordinated action. Moreover, the fact that an ideology cannot give instruction in what the leadership of a group of party should do cannot diminish the inconsonance of the decision of those who claim to be its adherents, but choose not to join on religious, moral, or legal grounds. By professing religious, moral, or legal scruples they merely profess their lack of ideological commitment. The serious adherent of an ideology is in the unique position of being compelled, if he is to be respected by his fellow adherents, of having to try to change human relationships, in the way that they have collectively decided, regardless of the fact that this may entail action to be judged sinful, wicked and criminal. Ideological commitment can be taken to preclude the relevance of commandments given, standards set and rules made in the world the committed propose to change. Their commitment may prove incompatible with religious, moral and legal obligations. The Marxist who argues that he has decided that he will not join a Marxist Party may have rejected the relationship he could have with his fellow adherents in favour of the relationship he has with other persons. In doing so he has rejected the relevance of his Marxism. His position is analogous to a man who professes his love for the wife of a friend, but refuses to make love with her because the act constitutes an adulterous betrayal. She may be entitled to conclude that, in the language of love, he speaks of a passion less ardent than hers. It is insufficiently decisive to motivate a change in the relationship between the three people immediately concerned.

Ideological conviction either justifies change in human relationships or it justifies nothing. Its vocabulary either constitutes the mode of communication between those prepared to become the members of a party or it makes no sense at all. The fact that it constitutes the language of a special relationship is alone commensurable with the fact that it can be taken to preclude talk of religious, moral and legal duties and obligations that relate the members of a party to other individuals outside it.

None the less, an ideology cannot permit an action in the way that the law legitimises an action which is not formally proscribed. It cannot place a man under an obligation to allow the instigation of an action (any more than it can demonstrate to him its efficacy in achieving a desired goal). It is not subscription to an ideology, but membership of the party which acts in the name of an ideology that obliges the adherents to accept the authenticity of a policy decision. That the claim to be an adherent of an ideology can be substantiated by the act of joining a group or party does not imply that the ideology has authorised the implementation of a particular policy. The rules of a group or party may facilitate that those who are adept in the business of leadership assume high office, and make their decisions binding on the other members, but an ideology has neither superiors nor subordinates, only adherents. They may refer to the sense it makes, to determine whether or not the justification given for adopting a proposal is orthodox, with some hope of success, but they cannot consult it with a view to deciding whether or not a policy is expedient. It is because 'political theories' do not translate into practice in this fashion that the formation of a party by those who subscribe to an ideology is an essential step towards their being able to rely upon their special relationships in effecting change. Without the formation of a disciplined party, the ideologically committed run the risk of being continually engaged in disputing what it is that their beliefs prescribe. In the absence of discipline the adherents of an ideology appear as suffering from the presence of too many chiefs and not enough Indians. The lack of a logical relationship between what the leaders of a group or party direct their followers to do, and the justification they give for doing it, increases, not decreases, the strength of their political relationship. Ideological argument cannot interfere with the recognition of the facts that those in office have authority, some are more experienced and gifted leaders than others, and there is a need for co-ordinated action. The same common, as distinct from ideological, sense that dictates that the ideologically committed arrange meetings also dictates that they do not behave as if they were members of a multi-party assembly.

Ideologically committed groups or parties are prone, as we know, to internal disputes, but these controversies cannot lead to the closing of ranks without those who promote them resorting to some procedure such as a vote, or by ordering a purge or heading a successful revolt. Differences about the 'correct way forward to communism', for example, cannot be resolved by an appeal to ideology. The members of a party may be in agreement as to how their programme of action is to be justified and be divided on what they should do. It is, however, understandable that once a prolonged conflict over policy has developed, different applications of the common ideological heritage will be devised. The separate applications are essential to the formation of separate camps. What expresses the fact that men legitimately enjoy the privileged relationships of group or party membership is not that they can all perceive how their policies are derived from their common beliefs, but rather the fact that they are able to reach binding decisions which they are happy to justify by reference to a set of beliefs. If it is apparent that they are divided, then we may expect to find that for practical reasons, the factions will devise different applications of their ideological tradition. Those who cannot agree upon, or accept, a policy must go their separate ways, and they cannot both justify the split in exactly the same way. The fact that political programmes cannot be derived from ideological visions of human relationships does not affect the fact that those who share them cannot have serious differences of opinion on policy without the party relationship affirmed in their ideological talk being threatened. At the same time, the fact that ideologies do not refer to the world facilitates their adaptation to justify changes of policy designed to revive confidence in a leadership which has been criticised by its rank and file. Let us now explore this interesting phenomenon.

The ideologically committed argue that there are grounds to justify our attempting to change human relationships regardless of the fact that those who, it is claimed, will benefit are not, at the present time, willing to admit that this is the case. Even Mill, one of the most reluctant to approve of paternalism, readily concedes that there are occasions on which the possibility of what he considers to be progress depends upon it. Liberals have accepted that it is impossible to force a man to be moral, but they have not rejected the claim that it may be desirable to change society in a way that will enable men to achieve a higher level of moral performance without their consent. They have not rejected it, because, like all classic ideologists, they believe themselves, unlike the common man, to be in possession of an understanding of the principles of correct political practice which places their practical judgement on a different plane from that of all those whose approach to political action is seen to be necessarily less professional.

The Marxist expects what he regards as a higher level of social consciousness from the 'communist' than from the 'capitalist', and the liberal expects a superior level of civilisation from those who live in a 'democracy' than from those subject to an 'oriental despot' or 'feudal lord'. Both believe that not only do they have 'philosophical' insight into the human condition, they also possess an understanding of the process of social, economic and political changes that places them in a position to engineer the creation of the form of human association most in accord with man's nature. Such an understanding, it is claimed, enables us to describe the conditions under which ideal society will materialise provided that their beneficial effect is not countered by perverse human intervention. Liberals inform us that when they come to power they will refrain from exercising the authority of their office to disrupt the arrangements which least hinder the psychological drive of every individual to improve his moral, intellectual, economic and political life. Marxists inform us that when they seize control of the machinery of state its power will be used to eliminate those conditions which arrest the completion of the historical process known as 'dialectical materialism' leading to the appearance of 'unalienated' man.

Now, given that statements of this kind are to be taken at their face-value, we might well expect the adherents of an ideology like liberalism or Marxism to break with the party they have seen fit to join, when progress towards the creation of ideal society does not, in spite of their efforts, seem to be taking place. This, however, does not appear to be the case. Liberals have claimed that, in Western Europe and America, the removal of restrictions on private enterprise, electoral reform and the provision of welfare by the state have not encouraged the development of the 'autonomous individual' they admire. It has encouraged the growth of organisations such as the 'industrial corporation', 'mass parties' and the 'bureaucratic state' which, they claim, suppress 'individualism'. Marxists too have asserted the failure of communist parties to effect the birth of the era of 'communist' man. Some have claimed that the seizure of the power of the state by communist parties has led, not to the creation of 'communist' society, but to the triumph of what they call 'state capitalism'. Nevertheless, they have sought to restate their ideological convictions rather than abandon what they conceive to be their ultimate goal. Since they could not derive their intentions in politics from their ideological convictions, they have not been rendered apolitical, or obliged to adopt the ideology of others, because their expectations have been disappointed. When they judge it inappropriate to go on justifying what they have done they can decide on a different strategy, and they can mark the break by devising a new version of their ideological vision. They can make it clear that they have, in terms of their identity, made a break with their past. The authoritative character of ideological writing no more precludes adaptation and innovation than the authoritative character of law precludes its modification. It is true that the intellectuals of an ideological movement cannot revise their theories to accommodate the fruits of unanticipated experience. Their theories do not, as we have seen, carry false information about the world to be corrected. They do not, as ideology, carry any information of this kind. However, they can be restated in the way that Lenin elaborated the Marxist thesis on the inevitable collapse of what he called 'capitalism' to show why, in Marxist–Leninist terms, a seizure of power by a para-military organisation, and not the intervention of the 'masses', which Marx called a 'revolution', was the way forward for communists in Russia. This adaptation was essential to the formation of the Bolshevik Party. Lenin effected it by giving an account of something called 'imperialism', as the final stage of 'capitalist' development, in which the 'exploitation' of colonial people afforded a temporary respite to the hitherto progressively impoverished European industrial workers. The respite is to be understood to have averted the 'revolutionary situation' envisaged by Marx. At the same time, the struggle for colonial possessions by the 'capitalist' states may be seen to involve them in exhaustive wars in which a power as ill-prepared as Russia may be expected to be one of the first to collapse. Its exhaustion is the opportunity for a small 'revolutionary' party to come to power and institute the required 'dictatorship of the proletariat' under which, it is claimed, the creation of the 'communist' society is possible.

Moreover, the fertile ideologist need never be confounded by the course of events. His interpretation of the political significance of the state of the world is not independent of what happens in it, but its status as part of an ideology is not dependent on what happens. An ideological thesis may turn out to have lost its relevance on account of a change of circumstances, but it cannot thereby be proved to be non-ideological or no longer to belong to a particular ideological tradition. Unless the actual policy of the Bolshevik Party could have been derived from Lenin's doctrines in 1917 its success could not prove that Lenin's 'theoretical' analysis is genuine ideology, any more than Hitler's final defeat proves that his version of racism is not genuine national socialism.

Ideologies are doctrines to which we can adhere. They are not, properly speaking, theories. We may believe in them; but we are not informed by them. Knowing what we believe in is not the same thing as believing that we know something. Doctrines which affirm that progress is the consequence of the conflict of ideas, classes, or races, and so on, take the form of the kind of theoretical understanding that is useful when we have to decide on the utility of alternative courses of action. However, although they have the form, they do not have the substance of theoretical knowledge. Just as ideological arguments cannot specify that a class of actions is legitimate or illegitimate, in the way that the law can permit and proscribe, they cannot demonstrate that, given we desire a particular result, this and not that is the way to secure it. The active adherent of an ideology will derive a political identity from the views he holds, but he cannot derive any professional expertise from them. His political decisions cannot command any respect from the fact that he justifies taking them in ideological terms. Marxists are obliged to recognise that, as an authority on Marxism in Marxist circles, whatever Lenin decided to do, the way he chose to justify his decision in Marxist terms is the correct way, but in so far as Lenin's actual decisions commanded respect, they did so because he was the founder and successful leader of the Bolshevik Party. No one can command support for Lenin's decisions by trying to demonstrate that they came from his having followed the procedure required to effect a desirable result for which Marxism gives the technical specification.

However, although we may succeed in refuting the claim of an ideologist that he possesses a knowledge of the conditions under which desirable economic and political development will occur, this cannot render him politically impotent. The relationship between his commitment and his forming, or joining, a party of like-minded adherents cannot be impaired by the fact that his pursuit of political objectives cannot be conceived as the application of principles or the findings of experimental inquiry. His political success may be incapable of proving his theories correct, but his political success is still possible provided that he contends in the political arena. Indeed the possibility of his succeeding there depends, in part, upon his ideological fertility. The fact that Lenin was an authority in Marxism is directly related to the fact that he came to hold an auhoritative office in the Soviet Communist Party.

The success of Oakeshott's attack on rationalism and Popper's attack on holism is achieved at the expense of a satisfactory account of the place of ideological argument in political life. It incorporates precisely the category mistake which precludes our recognising the sense made by ideological talk. In challenging the educational value of ideological instruction they have judged it according to the standards required of technical instruction in the application of rules and principles appropriate to guiding the use of factual information in reaching conclusions and making decisions. Having found it wanting as a member of this department of knowledge, they have rejected not only the claim that it is technical in the ways that laboratory training and meteorological instruction are technical, they have rejected the possibility that it has anything to do with a particular technique. Clearly, they do not consider that there is any aspect of political activity which cannot be conducted without an education in the use of ideological terms. Nowhere do they consider that an ideology offers instruction in the language in which we can affirm the identity required to enter into the special relationship between the committed members of a group or party.

The fact that it is clear that ideological talk is not instructive about doing something in the world does not preclude the possibility that it is about being in a relationship in it. The relationship of means to ends is not the only relationship characteristic of political activity. In the same way that lovers have a special relationship so do the committed members of a group or party have an exclusive tie. Although the former, unlike the latter, relationship is not a purposive association, in both cases the constant reaffirmation of the relationship in terms peculiar to the bond is essential to its durability. There appears to be noting that lovers can do together that those not in love cannot do once we deny the distinction between, for example, making love and enjoying sex. The distinction, however, is there. Making love is creating or affirming a relationship, it is not the pursuit of a sensation. The love relationship can, of course, be abused. And, just as the commitment of the lover can be exploited so can ideological commitment be made to serve a purpose. Anybody can join an ideologically committed group or party with what its serious members must regard as ulterior motives, and, on the face of it, successfully perform all we associate with group or party discipline. Their holding group or party membership no more guarantees ideological conviction, and the relationship established through its communication, than a marriage certificate guarantees that the married are bound by shared affection. However, those who are not in love, or ideologically committed, cannot convince themselves that there is anything to be said in the vocabulary of love or ideological conviction, respectively, which is not misleading. Those outside a relationship of love may well find it difficult to appreciate what it is that those who are in love find rewarding in one another's company, and those who do not share the same ideological conviction may well find it difficult to understand the satisfaction that those who do share it find in their group or party activity. The situation could hardly be otherwise. The satisfaction derived from exclusive relationships of this kind is not something that can be shown to be the result of something all men can desire such as sexual intercourse or power. It is intrinsic, not extrinsic, to the special relationship involved. It is not the result of the performance of any particular act the ideologically committed may decide upon, but the fact that it is they who perform it, that makes it worthwhile. The terms of ideological commitment make sense independently of those that refer to the relationship of means to ends. Talk of 'comradeship' and 'brotherhood' cannot in itself help the adherents of an ideology to create a new society and a new man, but it can invest their seizing power with a significance that other men cannot be expected to appreciate. The sense of the terms like 'revolution' and 'dictatorship of the proletariat' in Marxist literature cannot be translated into descriptive language. They are peculiar to affirming and reaffirming the relationship between adherents, not to declaring their objectives. On their being peculiar in this respect rests the claim that instruction in the ideological language to which they belong constitutes a preparation for political life.

The reason Oakeshott and Popper have made a mystery of why the ideologically committed have been able to invade the precincts of what they regard as the legally constituted citadel of civilised political practice, is that, in spite of the brilliance of their tactics, their strategy in attacking rationalism or holism is partly misconceived. The failure of ideology as the basis of an education in the selection of political goals or the identification of political opportunities is irrelevant to its success as instruction in the language of commitment. Ideological education is indispensable to authentic participation in the ritual of group or party meetings where the expression of solidarity and allegiance constitutes the *raison d'être* of the occasion. It would appear that Oakeshott and Popper have thrown the ideological baby out with the rationalist/holist bathwater. Ideologies that must be dismissed as academic nonsense can, after all, make political sense.

NOTES: CHAPTER 5

1 M. J. Oakeshott, *Rationalism in Politics* (Methuen, London, 1962).
2 K. R. Popper, *The Poverty of Historicism* (Routledge & Kegan Paul, London, 1957).
3 M. J. Oakeshott, op. cit., p. 31.
4 K. R. Popper, op. cit., p. 84.
5 ibid., p. 159.

6
The Uses of Ideological Language

'Can it be denied', thundered Matthew Arnold, 'that to live in a society of equals tends in general to make a man's spirits expand and his faculties work easily and actively?'[1] It can hardly have escaped our notice that a whole body of literature exists to do precisely this. We learn from it that, whereas our hypothetical man's spirits may indeed expand under these circumstances, it will only be at the expense of his productive capacity, or his ability to innovate and adapt to unfamiliar situations, or to recognise those amongst his fellows who are fitted to occupy authoritative positions, or even to respect those political arrangements which alone protect his equality. At some point, at least, disaster is widely predicted to follow upon such an arrangement.

Arnold's essay is, of course, in the way of an introduction to his studies of education, studies which he imagines provide evidence for such an assertion, or at least the kind of ground upon which any refutation is to be made. Yet any cursory examination of the arguments from the opposing camps will show that they arrive at their own conclusions on evidence, or even by methods, which pass by anything Arnold considers to support his own case. Are they even arguing about the same things? Faced with such a problem it is tempting to discount these assertions and counter-assertions as vapid or even nonsensical. It is to argue, in effect, that both Arnold and his opponents are not really referring to anything at all when expressions like 'equality' and 'the human spirit' are bandied about in this fashion. At the very least, it seems that they are vulnerable to the argument that their assertions are cast in an inappropriate form, for example, that of a scientific hypothesis or historical narrative. The question thus arises, if an argument of the kind in question cannot be supported in the manner that its author seems to suppose that it might, is it therefore worthless? If not, what might it achieve?

One kind of investigation which has been put forward as a means of answering just this kind of question is known as the history of political thought, and I shall consider that formulation of the latter study proposed by Professor Pocock. I refer to the account given in Pocock's essay 'Languages and their implications'.[2] Here Pocock would have us believe that statements like Arnold's are to be treated as discrete utterances, but also that we should adhere to the 'historically correct principle' that 'the interpreter's aim should be to present the text as it bore meaning in the mind of the author, or his contemporary reared'.[3] Our problem with Arnold, it is alleged, is to discover the particular linguistic paradigms within which Arnold spoke and within which his adversaries replied; then our problem of meaning will be resolved. Since part of my thesis bears a superficial resemblance to one formulation of Pocock's position, I propose to distinguish it at once by showing the incoherence of Pocock's account. This demonstration will have the dual purpose of showing that what is required is not a historical investigation but a philosophical one, and that this is not just relevant to our own particular problem as outlined above, but of more general significance for the very possibility of studying ideological argument historically.

Pocock argues that 'men think by communicating language systems'[4] and that each thought can thus be viewed as an event, as a moment in the transformation of a language system, and is thus amenable to historical treatment. It seems that at any one time there are many of these systems, or paradigms, in operation giving rise to the complex texture of political speech and resulting in the fact that men, in speaking, commit themselves to a 'load' of meaning which is beyond their control. The problem of control bulks large in Pocock's vision, for not only is he led to consider whether men might not be able to gain control of one or more paradigms and manipulate meaning, but he deals, in another essay, with the question of whether revolutions in linguistic paradigms must necessarily result in political revolutions.

There is, however, a basic error at the heart of Pocock's answer which renders all this elaboration nugatory. This error is most obvious when he persistently treats language, language-use, speech and meaning as if they were interchangeable. For men do not communicate language systems; if we must use this vocabulary they communicate *in* a language system, and our interest, and Pocock's too for that matter, lies both in *what* they communicate and the manner in which it is communicated. Both these concerns are not with language *per se*, but with its employment in specific instances, that is with language-use. Thus when Pocock claims that 'speech is a political operant . . . it invokes value, it summarises information, it suppresses the inconvenient, it makes many kinds of statement and does so by means of formulations which can often convey several kinds of statement at once, while simultaneously diverting attention from others',[5] we need to do some unravelling before we can arrive at a sensible formulation of his meaning. To begin with, there is, in his essay, a persistent confusion between utterances and language. People say things and they say things in a language. Invoking value, summarising information, and so on, are things that can be done in a language. Speech does not make many kinds of statements; people make many kinds of statements, which can, intentionally or otherwise, be open to all kinds of interpretations. If our concern is with meaning then we must be proficient in the language in which the statement is made. No one denies that the meaning of words sometimes changes, that, for example, Polybius did not mean the same thing when he used the word 'revolution' as Marx did. This, however, is a different matter altogether from the various interpretations and constructions which have been put upon a particular utterance, and the intended or unintended consequences which have attended it. Our investigation into the meaning of the word 'revolution' in a particular text is not historical just by virtue of the fact that the text was written in the past. As we shall see, the place to pursue our investigation into this problem is a good dictionary.

Furthermore, Pocock seems to think that such an investigation could proceed by producing hypotheses capable of falsification. Of course he is utterly unable to produce a single example of such a hypothesis being falsified. These hypotheses are supposed to be derived from a reconstruction of the linguistic paradigm, the 'mode of thought', of people in the past. Of course, all that has been done is to produce an *interpretation* of, for example, Burke, or ancient Chinese thinkers, with appropriate illustrations. It may be more or less plausible, helpful, or aesthetically pleasing, or may satisfy some other similar criteria, but there is no possible evidence that could falsify it, because neither the sense of statements nor the force of utterances (whichever Pocock wants) are derived from a 'paradigm' the application of which merely determines the identity of a particular discourse.

This brings us to Pocock's consequent error. If we are concerned with utterances we are concerned with statements made in a particular context. This is perhaps where talk of paradigms could be useful, for in science, they do permit a grasp on the relationship between language and the world, the relationship between the language we communicate in and the kind of things we can communicate about. However, the position in science is in no way analogous to that in politics. In the former we have a carefully circumscribed investigation which *is* the paradigm. Pocock is not just talking about political theory (and in any case we have seen that this is not a legitimate form of investigation) but about political utterances. Here the practice is politics itself, not an investigation, and the notion of a paradigm gets no grip at all. Here Pocock is doubly confused when he talks about different kinds of utterances deceiving, cajoling, exhorting, indeed all the activities of political rhetoric, as if they could be governed by different paradigms. If this is so, we are entitled to ask, what then makes them deceiving, cajoling, or exhorting? We must distance this from the notion of a tradition of discourse, which will be introduced below. The conservative and the liberal are both talking about politics, so they can respond to each other, unlike the alchemist and the modern scientist. Our concern with political utterances, then, will be semantic rather than epistemological. Thus we have seen how Pocock persistently confuses the meanings of statements with the consequences of utterances. This is at the root of the curious idea that each statement carries a 'load' of meanings which is beyond our control. It is not the meaning of a statement which we make which is beyond our control, or else we could never mean anything, but the consequences of uttering it in any particular context.

Our problem with Arnold and his critics is a very different one from that envisaged by Pocock; it is one of the meanings of the statements themselves. There is nothing in the past which could be evidence for the meaning of a statement, as there could be for the force of an utterance. At the level of meaning Pocock's mistake is to confuse meaning with interpretation. We are not concerned with the various interpretations which may or may not have been made of Arnold's statement except in so far as they provide further examples of ideological argument. That is, we are concerned to discover the particular kind of language-use in which these statements could communicate something, the particular *form* of utterance we are pointing to when we speak of ideology. This is not a historical investigation, because we have all that we need to hand: there is nothing other than the statements themselves which could constitute evidence for this or that form. We conclude, then, both that our inquiry is philosophical, and that by turning our backs on history we have not ignored an alternative and possibly more fruitful line of investigation.

If we are to attempt to locate the realm of application of ideological argument in political practice rather than as a theoretical investigation, we must begin by distinguishing between it and two other kinds of practical argument, moral and technical. Technical argument is essentially the demonstration of the manner in which a proposed course of action fulfils criteria which add up to its being the most rational means to a given end, and is absolutely dependent upon that end being the kind of goal to which techniques are applicable. Only then can the means stand in a technical relation to the end. If the goal is to move from A to B in the shortest time, then, by taking account of distance, gradients, terrain, and so on, the most efficient route can be planned given the information available. This latter *caveat* becomes of crucial importance when technical considerations are applied to future courses of action which may be affected by the actions of others, considerations which are relevant to political practice. Various more or less complex procedures for arriving at a technical conclusion here have been developed, game theory and decision theory, for example, but the fact that human conduct recognises considerations other than those of technical efficiency strictly circumscribes the range of problems to which they are applicable, a fact regrettably overlooked by some of their more devoted proponents.

Amongst these other considerations, those of morality are perhaps pre-eminent. Our making moral judgements derives from our perceiving a complex of duties and obligations, by virtue of our learning a language in which they have reference. Hence, whereas to justify a course of action on technical grounds may require that its efficiency be displayed, justification and condemnation on moral grounds does not proceed in the same way. Moral arguments *per se*, as opposed to arguments about morality, do not exist. The judgement that something is a lie is a matter of establishing that it is an untruth told with intent to deceive and condemnation follows; argument as to whether lying is wrong is of a totally different order. Moral and immoral men alike are confronted by the objective nature of moral judgement. As Hegel says, paraphrasing Aristotle, ' "an ignorant choice" between good and evil "is the cause not of the actions being involuntary" (of its being non-imputable) "but only of its being wicked" '.[6]

The desire to seek justification for a moral language, though misguided, has been as popular a project as the deeply felt need to find a justification for induction. However, it remains the case that neither science nor specific moral practices are one whit more nor less secure whatever the supposed achievements of either of these tasks. For whereas the individual practitioner may feel more secure in his own mind as a result of these various justifications, for example, he will not lie because he believes that lying does not promote the general happiness, this has not altered the meaning of 'lie'. Although there are close analogies between moral and ideological talk, particularly in the attribution of value, the crucial difference remains that the latter is a genuine species of argument, although we have not as yet discerned the grounds on which such an argument might be concluded. The practice of making moral judgements would simply be impossible without a broad consensus of opinion about the scope of these judgements, and this reduces moralising to a peripheral status. In our talk about politics we do not so much attribute value to actions or procedures, as attribute character. Making these characterisations stick, and clarifying the consequences of producing them, is the concern of ideological argument.

To illustrate the distinctions which have been drawn, consider the following passages from R. H. Tawney's essay 'The nationalisation of the coal industry'. Throughout the essay Tawney characteristically produces a host of technical arguments which are intended to point to the alleged efficiency of central planning over unsupervised chaos; the efficient use of resources for transport, drainage, exploration, marketing, and so on. It might be said to be a typically socialist preoccupation, of which more will be said later. However, Tawney also gives at least one moral justification; safety will be improved, he suggests, and 'it is reasonable to expect that the nation will obtain its coal without killing between three and four miners every day, and injuring 160,000 every year'.[7] Of course, as we have noted above, it is characteristic of moral judgement that it is not required that the point be clinched by concluding that killing miners is a bad thing and therefore . . . For it is open to an opponent to argue that such a state of affairs is of no importance; if he is to assume the offensive, it must be along the lines that this is an occupational hazard of mining and regrettably will not be changed by tinkering with ownership. But, in Tawney's view at least, the whole system is 'morally indefensible and professionally incompetent'.

The vital issue, to his mind, is not really this, however, for he wants to persuade us that the moral and professional shortcomings of the mineowners are merely symptomatic of a wider problem, that is, 'capitalist society'. 'It involves the treatment of human beings as part of the apparatus of production, instead of as the end for which it is worthwhile to carry on production at all . . . It is, in short, the enemy of freedom.'[8] This is an ideological argument, but those who would conclude that, as such, it is nonsense, should hesitate. It is true that, as quoted, out of context, we, the non-ideological readers, may be unable to specify what counts as treating a human being as part of the 'apparatus of production', let alone why this should be condemned in the same way that we might condemn treating human beings as animals. However, we should not ignore the fact that this is just what Tawney has been trying to show us in the rest of the essay; for example, counting the worker's life less than a small increment in profits. Obviously this is not like establishing the conclusion of a technical argument, and there is an objection that Tawney seems to think that it is, or else thinks that condemnation follows self-evidently as in moral argument. Certainly the form of much socialist argument is guilty of precisely this smudging of boundaries, a failing that lays it wide open to the Oakeshottian charge of rationalism. But to stop there is to miss the main drift of what has happened. It is not only for socialists that Tawney has succeeded in showing why certain procedures and their alleged consequences are things to be disapproved of. The ideological response to Tawney is not Oakeshott's. The old-fashioned liberal, for example, accepts that Tawney has given sense to the phrase 'treating the human being as part of the apparatus of production' but denies that this outcome is a consequence of these arrangements, or stresses the greater good that is to be derived from them.

Thus we see that what the ideologist has succeeded in doing is characterising events and practices. By reading his text we can come to see the sense in which a human might be treated as part of the 'apparatus of production', and presumably not as a human being. We do this by being able to list those things which are to count as examples of such treatment, and acceding to their force. Obviously the ideologist does not work in a vacuum, so there is a good stock of examples to draw from. His text finds its inspiration in everyday talk about politics, or other practices; talk about grievances, about improvements, which achieves a degree of sophistication not often recognised in accounts of the language of politics.

It will doubtless be objected here that non-ideological talk about economic or political practices is obviously couched in moral or technical language, which is precisely what this account has taken pains to distinguish from ideology. It might be argued, for example, that the force of Tawney's remark about the mistreatment of workers lies in the moral realm, and no more needs to be said other than to comment on his rather roundabout way of making the point. Such an objection misses the sense in which Tawney's claim is distinctively ideological. Whereas we can see at once the superiority of an arrangement which saves lives, what is the meaning, let alone the force, of his labelling a practice 'capitalist'? When he gives an account of a particular historical form of economic organisation and makes his charge about the treatment of human beings, it is difficult to see how he could be simply redescribing a practice, as we might, for example, on receipt of further information, redescribe a set of bodily movements such as digging coal or signing a contract. Although analogies have been drawn between Tawney's introducing the phrase to us, and our learning to use any new words or phrase, and it has been emphasised how ideological argument drew upon ordinary political language, the distinctions are clear. In the two examples given, there is a basic human agreement about what is to count as digging, and procedures for signing a contract are laid down in law; here philosophical investigation ends. What we lack are criteria for the application of terms like 'capitalism', used ideologically, of the kinds that we do have for descriptive terms in ordinary language. It is most curious, one might almost call it sophistry, to suggest that these ideological terms are *like* descriptions, only their criteria change from day to day.

What kind of criteria are these, that can so change? Let us try to imagine a world in which the names of physical objects were transposed at will, and to describe it we would say that the names lacked criteria for their application.

Tawney's essay is very restrained in tone and, on the surface, appears to circumvent these difficulties. He has, as we noted above, skilfully used examples to fill out his ideological conclusions for the benefit of those who might not be familiar with the phrase in question, but in fact its meaning is by no means settled. Are we to apply the appellation 'capitalist' only to those practices which have a certain set of legal arrangements, or, as some socialists argue to this day, will public ownership do little to alleviate the real problem? Given Tawney's account, now betraying its age (in terms of the language of socialism, of course, not in relation to any events which might be considered to have a bearing on the problem), it would seem that the particular arrangement of property that he calls 'capitalist' stands in a critical relation to the use of the phrase, and hence is non-ideological, as an economic historian might use it, for example. However, the same essay offers us another approach which concentrates on symptoms, and these are none other than the examples of mistreatment, waste, mismanagement, and so on, to which I have already referred. Now, those socialists who have noted that these symptoms are still present in those societies called socialist on the basis of their property arrangements have sought to withhold from them the label 'socialist' and substitute something like 'state-capitalist'. Here 'capitalism' no longer refers to the arrangement of property, as Tawney seemed to use it (thus earning the criticism of Marxists), but is, quite clearly, an ideological usage, for we can no longer tell unaided to what it refers, nor to what it might refer in the future. The best we can hope to find is an enumeration of those procedures which are now deemed to be 'capitalistic' in the works of an acknowledged socialist. Of course, this latter treatment is implicit in Tawney's essay, or its force as a statement of socialist outrage would be lost. By now, it seems, any analogy between Tawney's account of the treatment of certain human beings and ordinary descriptive words and phrases is lost.

We face what seems to be a paradox. Although there are broad limits to what could count as treating human beings as part of the 'apparatus of production', 'threatening liberty', 'breaking down traditional authority', and so on, within these limits there is a great deal of latitude. Much more so than in other kinds of talk. If the criterial relation of names to physical objects is inappropriate for ideological terms, so also is the concept of judgement. For determining whether a particular event or procedure is a revolution or revolutionary is not like the application of a rule to a specific event to discover whether

98 *The Form of Ideology*

it is an occasion for the application of this or that concept. Once again, the rule itself is lacking. Rather, as we shall see below, the mere announcement that such and such an event is a revolution sets it up to be seriously considered as such, as yet another example to be taken account of. Not only the circumstances themselves but also the contingently authoritative nature of the pronouncement, that it is made by an acknowledged expert in the particular tradition of discourse, for example, is to be taken into account when assessing an individual application of an ideological term. Rather than the application of a rule or standard, it looks as though something more creative, like interpretation, is appropriate here. Hence the phenomenon that innovation in a tradition of ideological discourse does not bear a necessary relation to the facts to which it might be a response, and that of the invulnerability of ideological arguments, whatever their form, to falsification in the manner of science. It must be emphasised that this is not a criticism of ideological discourse on the lines of Popper, except where ideologists themselves, especially Marxists, have conceived of their enterprise in this fashion. It is merely intended to point to the distinctions between ideological argument and other kinds of discourse.

It may be objected here that the way in which ideological arguments are actually conducted seems to bear little relation to 'interpretation'. However, as we have already pointed out, whatever the form of ideological arguments, these reflect not so much the logical status of the argument, but the varied respect with which other forms of argument have been regarded by different traditions. Thus, if philosophy is regarded as some kind of special investigation into the nature of ultimate reality, then we may expect ideologists to turn their attention to epistemological considerations in the hope of discovering things about the world, though of course the force of their arguments will remain practical. Their disappointment with 'conventional philosophy' will then be made clear as in Marx's reading of Hegel, for example. This is part of a venerable line in the ideological treatment of philosophy which finds a contemporary voice in Gidden's spurious puzzlement over some of Wittgenstein's early speculations on solipsism: 'A paralysis of political [*sic*] will appears in Wittgenstein's own diaries and lectures, e.g., "I cannot bend the happenings of the world to my will: I am completely powerless. I can only make myself independent of the world – and so in a certain sense master it – by renouncing any influence on happenings".'[9] Again, if the ideologist conceives of science as giving access to this special kind of knowledge, then we find a similar preoccupation with scientific method.

Whatever the form, however, we have seen that the project of the ideologist is not that of investigation, however conceived, for he has no subject to investigate. His task is an imaginative one, that of creating and defending a character for the practices he is concerned to influence. Barred on semantic grounds from description or judgement, and on epistemological grounds from explanation, ideological argument is an attempt to draw the language of everyday practices into a picture in which every event or procedure is seen in the light of the whole. In the process new words and phrases are coined and old ones acquire new meanings. The world of 'capitalism', 'false consciousness', 'alienation', 'surplus value' and 'exploitation' is not the world of which we are aware when we engage in economic transactions and political procedures, a fact which Marx attempted to turn to his advantage. But, of course, neither is it hidden from our eyes like the scientist's world of forces and particles, merely awaiting the appropriate method of investigation to be revealed. It is created in the works of Marx, and elaborated in those of his acknowledged disciples; it is a picture which we are invited to accept as an account of the character of our practices, a picture which asks us to reject them having seen them for what they 'really' are. To argue then, with Popper or Oakeshott, that no kind of investigation could produce the conclusions of Marxism, or that there can be no distinctively Marxist way of acting, is to argue against the form of ideological argument rather than against its use. It necessarily fails to touch ideological traditions which do not have this preoccupation with scientific form and it overlooks the sense in which various procedures can and do acquire ideological labels. Having given an account of the nature of these labels, it remains to show the particular part they play in political life.

First, however, we must deal with a possible misunderstanding. This thesis may seem to have a certain resemblance to W. B. Gallie's 'Essentially contested concepts'.[10] However, Professor Gallie's attempt to distinguish between the essentially contested and the radically confused by adding special conditions which the former must fulfil (those he numbers VI and VII), particularly that 'the derivation of any such concept from an original exemplar whose authority is acknowledged by all contestant users of the concept', merely robs it of any usefulness. There is no possibility of such an exemplar, for 'concepts' like 'revolution' are elaborated by their application to different examples, and the examples themselves are the subject of contest; Marxists have contested the claim of almost every illegal overthrow of a regime to the title of 'revolution', including that of the Bolsheviks in 1917. Certainly the basis upon which this has been carried out has been the accounts of 'revolutions' and 'socialist societies' found in the works of Marx, Lenin and others, but the sense of these accounts changes with the different examples which are used to support the contesting versions. It is just this which distinguishes ideology from utopia, but it is the application to the examples themselves which is the subject of contest, there being neither rules nor criteria to allow any orderly procedures of adjudication to take place. But in no sense is the result radical confusion.

The features of ideological argument which allow us to distinguish it from moral or legal judgement are related to this point. From our account we have seen that the ideologist has not only to establish that something is, for example, a 'tradition' or a 'revolution', but also to show why his labelling the events in this manner constitutes a genuine characterisation, that is, why it is to be commended or deprecated. This is not to say that the two procedures are not closely related in actual argument; if they were not then the ideologist's close, but for our purposes misleading, concern with the manner in which his argument is presented would be pointless. It is the ability to create a character by what looks like description or judgement which is the peculiar feature of ideology. We notice particularly that a developed ideological tradition portrays each event, not in isolation, but as a manifestation of the whole. This is its pictorial quality. If it appears that there could be no event which could be excluded *a priori* from being a manifestation of 'class-consciousness' or fundamentally conditioned by man's ignorance of the consequences of his actions, then this is not a fault *per se*, but just a clue as to the genre of the picture we are considering. The disposition of the author is manifested in his images, but these images are not 'ways of seeing' in a popular phrase of social science, not the misunderstanding that hides objective reality, whatever that might be. For the picture is not a more or less distorted account of the practices themselves, like the student's incompetent figure study, but a sophisticated manner in which men have been accustomed to articulate their hopes and fears, desires and aversions when talking about politics.

What the ideologist requires above all, then, is creative imagination to draw upon contemporary themes and exhibit them in a coherent manner. When we speak of the ideological imagination, it should not be construed as implying that ideological conceptions are imaginary. This, as we have noted before, is the characteristic of a utopia: an imaginary state of affairs designed to point a moral by comparison with actual states of affairs. As such, 'utopian' is often an insult in ideological argument, as in Marx's castigation of the utopian socialists. A similar sense of 'imaginary' is to be found in children's stories and the literature of fantasy. Then, the objection continues, neither is the ideological imagination anything like our everyday use of the word, an invitation to see something as something else. If I were to imagine the reading room of the library to be the back bar of The Shakespeare Tavern for example, it might reconcile me to an afternoon's work. The objection continues that in this example I have no difficulty in describing both places in everyday language, both rooms are known to me by intimate aquaintance; but if I am invited to see this illegal assembly as a struggle for 'liberty' we are still left with the problem that we have neither rules nor criteria for deciding whether to object or concede to its being so characterised. In the objection this is supposed to be analogous to the case of the tone-deaf man claiming that he can imagine what it is like to have perfect pitch. These examples are very instructive. The fact that the tone-deaf man cannot take part in the practice of music and its associated language is not an empirical difficulty, as it would be the case that if I had never been to Durham I would not know what The Shakespeare Tavern was like. The tone-deaf man is, in Wittgenstein's phrase, *eo ipso* excluded from the world of music – 'there is something right about saying that unimaginability is a criterion for nonsensicality'.[11] There is a strong analogy here with the man who cannot think in ideological terms, whether it be some disability akin to tone-deafness (and such a disability, if it existed, would surely rule him out of political life), or a more or less successful shutting out by effort of will, as the judge who properly determines whether an assembly was illegal, or the historian who discovers what happened independent of its significance for him.

If I am invited to regard this action as furthering liberty, I can, if I am sensitive to ideological nuance, link the actions themselves to a picture of man and his place in the world. I might see him as requiring 'autonomy' to 'realise his nature', as divided into 'self-regarding and other-regarding persons', as having right to 'positive' and 'negative liberty'. It matters not that these terms first saw the light of day in utterly fatuous 'philosophical' speculations which are ultimately circular or nonsensical. It does matter that I should know that standing on a box at Hyde Park Corner is realising my 'autonomy', and a 'positive liberty', and that fighting the National Front in the street is a difficult dilemma that requires a 'philosopher' in All Souls or Harvard to reckon up some obscure calculus, given that these nasty people are plainly 'self-regarding', before I know what to do. The objection against regarding the ideological imagination as 'seeing-as' fails because ideological terms do have application and, more important, consequences for political life. It is true that I must have some introduction to ideological language and political practice before I can make an intelligent response, but not only is it clear that the language of politics is largely made up of such talk, but this 'entry condition' applies to any other language (by which is meant, for example, mathematical or moral language rather than French or German). We certainly shall puzzle over the meaning of ideological terms if we imagine that they arrive complete with their application out of the blue.

We can press the analogy with tone-deafness further still by showing how ideological language organises an area of experience so that an appropriate response can be made from within. The reply to the claim that this illegal assembly is a 'struggle for liberty' and hence should receive our support is one that can be made by all those who see the force of the remark, not just those who accept it. The response might be that as such it is a dangerous threat to 'traditional authority', and should be punished with the full severity of the law, or that, as mere 'putchism', it is a manifestation of the 'empiricist problematic of the subject' and the participants require a healthy dose of 'theoretical practice' to see the error of their ways. It is disingenuous to press the argument that these people really are not arguing about anything at all. The argument is about the ideological characterisation of events, actions and practices.

These characterisations have many consequences. The first and, it might be said with reason, the pre-eminent, is the concern with a style of engagement in practice. It is possible, for example, to develop a critical faculty for inappropriateness amongst both friends and enemies. The charge against Hayek's *Road to Serfdom* made by Oakeshott is of this order: 'a plan to resist all planning may be better than its opposite, but it belongs to the same style of politics'.[12] A most instructive example is to be found in Barrington Moore's essay 'Revolutionary and reactionary imagery' (to be found in his *Social Origins of Dictatorship and Democracy*).[13] His account, as its title indicates, is not drawn from outside the realms of ideological argument, but is a contribution to a particular genre. It cries out against a particular style of engagement, in the manner that makes socialism anathema to the conservative, and so comic to anyone with a sense of humour. 'Reactionary imagery', it is claimed, glorifies the amateur (a reflection of class interest, naturally), but although Moore allows that some good can be attributed to it, in itself a curious claim, it is eventually weighed and found wanting.

> In many circles among the gentry and upward, any attempt at conversation beyond sport and gardens is likely to evoke pained surprise and the suspicion that the speaker has 'Bolshie' tendencies. For every distinguished patron of the intellect, for every eccentric defender of unpopular causes, and certainly for every aristocrat who has used his independence as a stepping stone to real intellectual achievements, there are many empty and frivolous lives. For every Bertrand Russell, there are probably a score of Colonel Blimps.[14]

For when we speak of images, we are not merely concerned with imagery, the clenched fist and handshakes on the cover of Moore's book, but a manner of engagement articulated in the language of an ideological text. The idea that it is somehow disgraceful for those with means to dispose of them for their personal enjoyment is balanced by the distrust of the conservative for the man who admits to finding justification in dogma. It is of course for this reason even more galling for the socialist to find a rejection of his picture dressed up in his own favourite form, for example, the modern liberal version of *The Fable of the Bees* which sometimes passes for economic theory. However, whereas academic criticism can represent the form in which the picture is presented – it can show, as Popper, Oakeshott and others have done, that philosophy or science, theology or psychology cannot establish a conclusion of this kind – such criticism leaves the disposition which found its expression in the account, and hence its force, unchanged.

We discover, then, a close connection between those ideological texts which we have discussed and the picture of practices constructed from the images men have of the character of political and other relationships. It is this connection which preserves the identity of an ideological tradition, and ensures that the use of ideological terms will not be entirely arbitrary, as we were originally led to believe, but will be governed by that kind of standard which will allow of judgements such as appropriateness. Without a knowledge of the relevant standards there cannot even be the attempt, but it is the act of interpretation which is the central feature of the ideological imagination: the production of an argument which is distinctly socialist in character, for example, which takes account of how an event has altered the world and indicates to us how we should regard it. Of course, part of the art of interpretation involves appeal to various acknowledged masters of the tradition, so the identity is sustained. But the interpretations themselves are ever changing in response to the ideological imagination; hence to look for real or coherent or exemplary meanings of words like 'revolution', 'tradition', 'liberty', or 'nation', when these words appear in the context of an ideological argument, is mistaken. Equally mistaken is the idea, found in Gallie's paper, that continued debate about these works will refine their meaning and move towards a consensus. For it is incumbent upon the ideologist to show us how *he* is using a word, and up to the adherent to decide whether this is a genuine or fraudulent use of it, a development or a perversion of the tradition of discourse.

The analogy between the failure to develop ideological sensibility and tone-deafness should not, however, be pressed too far. It is characteristic of the imaginative nature of ideological argument that there are no limits other than stylistic, beyond which it does not make sense to use a figure of speech. Our analogy is of heuristic value only, to be dropped when it has outlived its usefulness. I do not propose to discuss the nature of tone-deafness here but there is a danger that, if it is construed only as a physical disability, then the corresponding sensitivity to musical nuance appears to be just a psychological capacity. On its own this may be a useful way of looking at the question, but it should not distract us from the fact that when we are considering the development of a critical faculty for appreciating music this is a faculty that is learnt as a practice, rather than as a piece of behaviour, and that it is not just articulated in, but in a sense limited by, the stock of appropriate judgements available. It is this latter aspect that allows us to pursue the analogy, if we wish, with the colloquial usage of tone-deafness. When we speak of someone's sensibility to ideological nuance, or his disposition to envisage politics as this kind of activity or that, we are not speaking of anything psychological, but of an ability to use language to link actions and procedures to various images of the manner in which these activities should be carried on. This whole essay could be seen as an attempt to distinguish the ideological 'should' from the moral or the technical.

To illuminate this account of ideological argument we shall consider some of the ways in which such a tradition does develop, and how it relates to events and practices. It has not escaped attention that the language of ideology is often picturesque and flamboyant; in particular it abounds with metaphor and other figurative uses of language. There is Bentham's 'political machine', Rousseau's 'man in chains', to say nothing of Popper's 'Open Society'. This is partly historical accident, for a whole group of texts studied as the classics of political literature, the works of Burke and Paine and their contemporaries, and the tradition of writing which includes Carlyle, Stephen and Maine, are constructed in a style in which the well-turned metaphor is an essential part of the argument. This itself is obviously related to the Aristotelian notion of the place of metaphor in the art of rhetoric. However, by examining just how the metaphor enters the argument and its place in concluding it, we are able to learn much about the nature of ideology.

It has been suggested that ideological arguments are all to be understood metaphorically; all talk of social justice, natural rights, contracts and compacts are nonsense if taken literally, but saved if understood metaphorically. The sense of metaphorical or figurative here is found in Professor Strawson's essay 'Categories' and is related to the temptation to treat ideological argument as a huge category mistake: 'it is often remarked that category absurd sentences, though they resist literal interpretation, frequently lend themselves to figurative interpretation . . . [we] bring the categorically absurd in from the cold of the blankly nonsensical to the wide and welcoming domain of figurative speech'.[15] Once again, however, Strawson's own warnings about the indiscriminate use of the concept of category mistake aside, the objector who brings Rylean notions about categories to bear upon ideology is guilty of mistaking the form for its substance. Worse, he cannot then save ideology, as was his intention, by bringing it into 'the wide and welcoming domain of figurative speech'. For the meaning of a metaphor is discovered or displayed by cashing it out in literal terms and, unlike our own account, the ideology-as-metaphor thesis begins precisely from the premise that ideology taken literally is nonsense. At the root of this mistake is a muddled notion of the meaning of metaphor, one that invests it with a kind of magical potency by denying that a metaphor can be reduced to a set of literal statements.

Max Black provides a particularly clear example of this mistake. On his account the metaphor involves 'an interaction between the terms of its formulation' to produce a 'cognitive content'.

> Suppose we try to state the cognitive content of an interaction metaphor in plain language . . . the set of literal statements so obtained will not have the same power to inform and enlighten as the original. For one thing, the implications previously left for a suitable reader to adduce for himself with a nice feeling for their relative priorities and degrees of importance are now presented explicitly as though having equal weight. The literal paraphrase inevitably says too much and with the wrong emphasis.[16]

Perhaps the confusions of this account can be traced to the idea that meaning is a 'cognitive content', possibly some set of mental images experienced by the reader. Certainly his account of the inadequacy of the literal paraphrase is very weak. How does a suitable reader go about adducing the implications at all, we are surely entitled to ask, unless it is by using the large stock of words which exist to express relative priorities and degrees of importance? His grasp of the vocabulary is precisely his qualification for the description of 'a suitable reader'.

Behind this kind of talk is the idea that metaphors and other figures of speech articulate an experience, and understanding the meaning is equivalent to having the same experience. This is, of course, related to the whole notion of meaning and understanding being the same thing as experiences, and language existing to transmit these things between persons. Then it seems that some linguistic forms are more expressive than others, in the sense of more meaningful, notably poetic metaphor. But of course, powerful arguments have been brought to bear against the whole notion of meaning and understanding as experiences, most notably by Wittgenstein.[17] This is not to deny that certain kinds of discourse, especially poetic, may be associated with the production of images, and that these may have a special role to play, but whatever this role is, it cannot be that of meaning.

Black's account misses the sense in which a badly constructed figure can be inappropriate for, as the figure changed, on his account the 'cognitive content' would presumably change also. Instead we should concentrate our attention on what it is that is expressed by the metaphor and then we can proceed to the task of the literary critic, deciding whether it is expressed appropriately or not. The concept of meaning as interaction simply destroys this possibility. As Adam Smith put it:

> [Tropes and figures] give no beauty of their own; they are only agreeable and beautiful when they suit the sentiment, and express in the neatest manner the way in which the speaker is affected. When the common form of speech well enough describes what we want to make known, or sufficiently communicates our sentiments yet perhaps it does not express clearly and with sufficient life the manner we ourselves regard it – if in this case the figurative way of speaking is more suited to our purpose, then it surely ought to be used preferably to the other.[18]

His idea that a metaphor in fact tells us something about the manner in which the author regards his subject matter will be discussed below.

We should, therefore, be suitably critical about distinguishing between the figurative and the literal, and eschew general theories of metaphor and ideology. The analogy which tempted these theories in fact lies with the creativity of poetic metaphor, the poet's ability to use apt, yet novel and startling, characterisations of the everyday world. A good deal of discussion of poetic metaphor has centred on the question of whether metaphor refers in a strict sense. The whole problem, like that we encountered above, comes from conceiving metaphor as a wayward attempt at description. M. B. Hester, who does not quite escape this himself, correctly concludes that strict notions of truth and falsity are inappropriate and suggests the happy compromise of verisimilitude, taken to mean in this context that the metaphor expresses something about its subject that strikes the reader as being singularly appropriate.[19]

Whereas in poetry our appreciation of poetic metaphor is governed by the conventions of Western poetic construction, which is something which can be acquired, our talk about politics is not exactly of the same order. Professor Strawson touched exactly on this point when he discussed the ethical imagination being captured by dramatic statements expressing ethical pictures, 'profound truths' as he calls them. 'It is certainly possible in a coolly analytical frame of mind, to mock at the whole notion of a profound truth, but we are guilty of mildly bad faith if we do.'[20] Political ideology creates a context in which it makes sense to see some truths as more profound than others, and a metaphor is a particularly stylish way of doing it. Of course a good deal of weight now rests upon the individual adherent and his capacity to accept the profundity of the ideologist's characterisations, as well as upon the ideologist's capacity to give them suitable expression, but this is as it should be. Before we consider the consequences of this account for political practice, it is instructive to lay out an example of the place of metaphor in ideological argument.

Metaphor, then, is an important brush in the ideologist's paintbox, filling in the picture with a broad sweep, creating connections with the range of associations which a well-turned metaphor has at its disposal. We should not be surprised that ideologists are sometimes wary of allowing the reader too much latitude in further interpretation of these associations, but press on themselves to extend the metaphor, producing those characteristic passages where the ideological vision is, paradoxically, at its most direct. Here is Burke elaborating a disposition towards change in the world:

> When I see the spirit of liberty in action, I see a strong principle at work: and this for a while is all that I can possibly know of it. The wild *gas*, the fixed air is plainly broke loose: but we ought to suspend our judgement until the first effervescence is a little subsided, until the liquor is cleared, and until we see something deeper than an agitation of a troubled and frothy surface. I must be tolerably sure before I venture publicly to congratulate men upon a blessing that they have really received one . . . the effect of liberty to individuals is that they may do what they please. We ought to see what it will please them to do before we risk congratulations which may soon be turned into complaints.[21]

If we are not familiar with the language we may puzzle a little over the 'spirit of liberty', but the penultimate sentence gives us a pragmatic account. The heart of the passage is obviously the extended metaphor. A picture of men doing as they please is created; they are to be regarded carefully, even a little dubiously, for 'wild gas broke loose' is hardly a comforting thought. Burke lets us know elsewhere how he thinks men should go about changing their world, but it is quite clear just from this passage that this is not the way.

For those who can admire such a picture it is nicely put; for those that cannot it obviously strikes a jarring note.

> As to the tragic painting by which Mr. Burke has outraged his own imagination, and seeks to work upon that of his readers, they are very well calculated for theatrical representation, where facts are

manufactured for the sake of show, and accommodated to produce, through the weakness of sympathy, a weeping effect. But Mr. Burke should recollect that he is writing History not *Plays* and that his readers will expect truth, and not the spouting rant of high-toned explanation.[22]

Unfortunately for Paine, neither he nor his antagonist was writing history; they were characterising events, setting them in a coherent order, helping contemporaries to decide their attitude towards them, and we should not be at all surprised that Paine himself should appeal to the weakness of sympathy by theatrical representation.

It is properly from the elevated mind of France, that the folly of titles has fallen. It has outgrown the baby-clothes of *Count* and *Duke* and breached itself in manhood. France has not levelled it has exalted . . . The punyism of senseless words like *Duke* and *Count* or *Earl*, has ceased to please. Even those who possessed them have disowned the gibberish, and as they outgrew the ricketts have despised the rattle . . . Titles are like circles drawn by the magicians wand to contract the sphere of man's felicity. He lives immured within the Bastille of a word, and surveys at a distance the life of men.[23]

Between those who can see titles as baby-clothes and those who can take comfort in the 'shading oak' of the aristocracy there is a gulf which cannot be bridged by facts. What we have seen is the expression of dispositions, a difference between those who see the past as something they outgrew, and throw down its institutions like the baby's rattle, and those who believe that 'People will not look forward to posterity who never look backward to their ancestors'.[24] We have seen how metaphor, in the hands of consummate artists, can express profound truths.

Returning to our investigation of the nature of ideological argument, it could be argued at this point that these characterisations, which I have concluded are the outcome of ideological argument, are politically impotent. That is, since politics is a practice which is pre-eminently concerned with action, the ideologist is merely superficial, clever in his imaginative constructions no doubt, but bearing much the same relation to those engaged in the practice as the railway artist does to the engine-driver. This is to have missed the point. As was emphasised at the beginning of this chapter, ideological argument is a pervasive manner of speaking about politics, used by people engaged in the practice. It is up to us to discover its life. To begin with, as we have already noted, ideology is intimately connected with style, and a style of acting as well as speaking. In so far as the ideologist has persuaded people to conceive of their activities as a 'struggle for liberty', or a 'resurgence of the national spirit', or a 'long march to communism', then we can expect different styles of politics to emerge. This is particularly clearly shown in the connection between military imagery and revolutionary socialist parties, and cleverly articulated in Lenin's extended metaphor in *What Is To Be Done?* comparing the revolutionary party to a band of armed men on a cliff face, surrounded by swamps, and fired on from all sides.[25]

It is true that, lacking criteria for their application, it is difficult to see how well-formed intentions can be articulated in ideological terms, for we do not thereby indicate a specific course of action. The creativity of the ideologist, his power to evoke approval or condemnation, to inspire hope, fear or content, is purchased at a certain cost. To 'destroy creativity', to 'fight for freedom', to 'purify the race', or to 'overthrow capitalist society' are not descriptions of actions, and should not be assessed as such. But they are characterisations of actions; men have been persuaded to see their activities as falling under one of these heads, and they have been brought to see the force of justifications given in this language.

It might be objected that this lack of criteria means that nothing whatever can be *communicated*, certainly not a set of arrangements like a vision of a new society. What does a socialist society consist in? It has been argued that because, if pressed, the socialist must retreat into the dim recesses of his picture and come up with something like a society of 'unalienated men', or men with a 'new consciousness', he has lapsed into nonsense; that nothing could count as changing man's consciousness because we are unable to give a sensible formulation of what this kind of consciousness is in the first place. If, and this is all too often the case amongst socialists, the exercise is conceived of as deriving from some social science which will give us access to the consciousness of the epoch, we must reluctantly agree; but note that we have fallen back into academic criticism once again. In practice a Marxist would only talk like this to other Marxists where the possibility of such a study is already accepted. Even to the non-ideological reader the language of socialism indicates that in a future socialist society the arrangements will be different from those which we enjoy today, they will be more rational (that is, means-ends rationality will be applied to as many practices as possible as an ultimate value), differences of status, for example, which cannot be justified rationally will be overthrown, and so on. Thus does ideological argument get a hold on the world, in this very general orientation, related, as we have already noted, to dispositions amongst adherents to conceive of their world in this way or that.

In this manner socialists may dispute about whether any particular procedure is in accord with these principles; in doing so they are committed to academic nonsense, continuing to search for the cause of events, for example, but it remains distinctively *socialist* nonsense. The liberal can take fright that a procedure which the socialist has characterised as 'rational', a national economic plan, for example, threatens the 'liberty of the individual', understood in liberal terms. The attack may be dressed up in the most ill-fitting collection of theoretical garments – Hayek's attempt to show that economic planning is potentially disastrous in terms of a particular economic model, for example – but the force is unmistakable to anyone with ideological sensibility. At one level this explains the theoretical 'overkill' characteristic of ideological argument. If a theoretical investigaton, such as the kind of economic science which Hayek has in mind, could reveal the order of the market, then his demonstration that socialist planning contravenes this order, or that 'social justice is an empty phrase without determinable content', should allow him to sleep easy. However, what he has actually done, of course, is shown how those practices which socialists have claimed as their own contravene liberal aspirations and hence his further task is to prevent socialists from persuading liberal adherents or the uncommitted otherwise. At the other level, then, it gives us an insight into the nature of ideological argument, and shows it, appearances notwithstanding, to be firmly rooted in practice.

We have already seen how metaphor admirably suits the ideologist's purpose, but he can also coin neologisms to express his picture, terms like 'open society' or 'social justice', which are not strictly metaphorical but function in much the same way, by indicating, by association and through synonyms, those actual arrangements, procedures and actions which accord with its spirit. The 'open society' allows free discussion of ideas and is not 'closed to innovation' (which may be dressed up in a philosophical account of the progress of knowledge through falsification). Or at a more mundane level it is one which opens its borders and benefits from being a 'meeting point of culture'. Now, we can understand that for some people these things are not virtues at all, but for those whose ideas about how a society should be organised are broadly liberal in sympathy, it is profoundly apt. For those people the list of arrangements which accord with the disposition expressed by 'open society' are more all-embracing than my examples. There will, of course, be disagreement over some points, and these will be difficult to decide in a disciplined way, but this should not worry us unduly. It is after all not so much *what* is decided as the success that attends this decision in terms of persuasion amongst adherents and fellow travellers that is important.

We both can and should distinguish ideological argument from other kinds, and explore its limits, but we should not conclude that it is impotent because it is different from other well-defined modes of discourse. Competence in ideological argument allows us access to a vocabulary with which to express our practical concerns about political practice by referring to our visions of desired relationships and states of affairs. If the ideologist has a fault, it is his tendency to look upon political practice with contempt, as a sordid necessity which has to be tolerated. For it is the existence of politics which provides the material for the ideological imagination to work on. When Disraeli's Sidonia lectured the young Coningsby on politics he said, 'a political institution is a machine; the motive force is the national character. With that it rests whether the machine will benefit society or destroy it.'[26] This is merely the ideologist's conceit, for the motive force is the changing world created by human practices, and it is to this world that the ideologist responds.

NOTES: CHAPTER 6

1 Matthew Arnold, *Democratic Education*, ed. R. H. Super (University of Michigan Press, Ann Arbor, 1962), p. 8.
2 In J. G. A. Pocock, *Politics, Language and Time* (Methuen, London, 1972).
3 ibid., p. 6.
4 ibid., p. 15.
5 ibid., p. 18.
6 G. W. F. Hegel, *Philosophy of Right*, trans. T. M. Knox (Oxford University Press, London, 1967), p. 94.
7 R. M. Tawney, *The Radical Tradition* (Pelican, Harmondsworth, 1966), p. 131.
8 ibid., p. 142.
9 A. Giddens, *New Rules of Sociological Method* (Hutchinson, University Library, London, 1976), p. 166.
10 W. B. Gallie, 'Essentially contested concepts', *Proceedings of the Aristotelian Society*, vol. LVI, 1955–6, pp. 167–98.
11 L. Wittgenstein, *Zettel* (Blackwell, Oxford, 1967), para. 263.
12 M. J. Oakeshott, *Rationalism in Politics* (Methuen, London, 1962), p. 21.
13 Barrington Moore Jr, *Social Origins of Dictatorship and Democracy* (Penguin University Books, Harmondsworth, 1973).
14 ibid., p. 490.
15 P. F. Strawson, *Freedom and Resentment and Other Essays* (Methuen, London, 1974), p. 131.
16 Max Black, *Models and Metaphors* (Cornell University Press, New York, 1962), p. 44.
17 C. L. Wittgenstein, *Philosophical Investigation* (Blackwell, Oxford, 1974), paras 132–242.
18 Adam Smith, *Lectures on Rhetoric and Belles Lettres* (Nelson, London, 1963), p. 29.
19. M. B. Hester, *The Meaning of Poetic Metaphor* (Mouton, The Hague, 1967), p. 165.
20 P. F. Strawson, op. cit., pp. 28–9.

112 The Form of Ideology

21 Edmund Burke, *Reflections on the Revolution in France* (Pelican, Harmondsworth, 1968), pp. 90–9.
22 Thomas Paine, *Rights of Man* (Pelican, Harmondsworth, 1969), pp. 71–2.
23 ibid., p. 102.
24 Burke, op. cit., p. 119.
25 V. I. Lenin, *What Is To Be Done?*, ed. S. V. Utechin (Oxford University Press, London, 1963), p. 43.
26 B. Disraeli, *Coningsby* (Dent, Everyman's Library, London, 1971), p. 199.

Postscript

In a sense it is necessary that a book that is composed of the contributions of six authors should have a postscript. A conventional conclusion is inappropriate for two reasons: first, there is the practical reason that a conclusion is unlikely to do justice to the variety of arguments deployed in such a book and, secondly, it is the case that it is in the very nature of a philosophical investigation that the result does not lend itself to systematic formulation. It is in this sense that Wittgenstein claimed that 'my thoughts were soon crippled if I tried to force them on in any single direction against their natural inclination'.[1] This is not a textbook. It is intended to assist the reader achieve coherence in his thought about ideology, but he must achieve that coherence himself. This postscript cannot do more than encourage and aid the formation of further reflection on the form that ideology takes.

Chapter 1, 'Ideology and the Sociological Understanding', concludes that the sociological notion of ideology is seriously defective and it may be that the consequences of this are greater than they seem. The very term 'ideology' has gained what currency it possesses largely in the promotion of those sociological ideas which have proved erroneous. We cannot simply say, therefore, that *this* account of ideology is wrong but suppose all the while that a correct account of ideology remains to be given, for with the destruction of the sociological account (which is really a philosophical account presupposed by the sociology) it is not clear that there is anything left to be given an account of. The same is not true of, for example, a philosophical account of the nature of science because in this case we have an everyday understanding of what is and what is not to count as science embedded in our referential use of the term and one which is fairly well fixed. Consequently, should some one account of science prove unsatisfactory we may proceed, confident in the possibility of a true one. One of the ways we may set about constructing it is by attending to and trying to elicit the principles of the use of the word science in ordinary, non-problematic cases. The trouble with ideology, however, is that there are no unproblematic uses and there is no consistency in the way the term is employed from writer to writer. On the Marxist view, liberalism is ideological because it constitutes an uncritical endorsement of the *status quo*, a ruling illusion. To the liberal, Marxist talk is ideological because it is pseudo-theoretical and doctrinaire. To the Burkean conservative, liberalism and Marxism are equally ideological because both consist in 'recipes' for political success. Does the refutation of the sociological notion, then, not signal the end of any profitable study of ideology?

The proper answer to this reasonable question is boringly cautious: 'not necessarily'. The linguistic anarchy described above is not as total as might be supposed. Two vague but abiding features attach to almost all uses of the word ideology, and these may serve a useful purpose. First, it is generally agreed that ideology has something to do with political doctrines and theories. This by itself would not serve to distinguish it from, for example, political philosophy, but in the second place, it is agreed, by and large, that ideology has to do with universally, or at least not parochially, relevant beliefs of a non-prescriptive kind, but which nevertheless have practical import. Even taken together these two features do not supply much scope for constructive and critical thought but they do provide criteria sufficient for us to pick out a class of beliefs in the history of political thought and of works in which such beliefs are formulated and discussed, though, it is true, a class with very unclear borders. Still, with only this we may now proceed in something of an empirical manner, not by trying to find some empirical generalisations which are true of all those works, but by seeing whether, in the light of the aims and methods of those beliefs and their formulation, we can offer the rational construction and reconstruction of a form of thought and argument which, whether or not it is found extensively at work in the books with which we began, presents a possible understanding that has a certain degree of coherence and unity and which we may term ideology.

Two important remarks are to be made upon such an enterprise. First, because an account like this is partly critical and constructive it must, as all philosophical accounts must, depart from the actual to an extent which will leave it uncertain sometimes how far what is discussed is merely a possibility which the philosopher is pleased to call by the name he does. In most cases this danger, the danger of stipulative definition, is avoided by the appeal to ordinary language, but in the case of ideology, there is no ordinary language. Consequently, it will remain uncertain how far such an account as is envisaged here is an account *of ideology* in any important and meaningful sense. Secondly, we cannot assume, because an enterprise of this sort may be outlined, that it is guaranteed success. It may be that the beliefs and writings lumped together by the relatively vague criteria with which it is suggested we work present and suggest nothing whatever in the way of a uniform or coherent form of understanding but only a hotch-potch of this and that, whose classification under a single label will be uninterestingly arbitrary.

This is why, to the suggestion that the conclusions of the first chapter show 'ideology' to be a worthless concept, we can only answer 'not necessarily so'. To confirm or refute the suggestion further investigation must be undertaken and its outcome cannot be predicted in advance. It must be added, however, that should such an investigation confirm the suggestion, it does not follow that it has been a waste of time.

Chapter Two, 'Religion and Ideology', expresses dissatisfaction with two views of the relationship between religious belief and adherence to an ideology. Given the variety of both, this seems an ambitious project, so it is not surprising that religion is construed as referring to Christianity, and mainstream Christianty at that. There may be, of course, Christian sects that do not appear to be covered in the exposition given here. What can be intelligently said about them would then depend on the concepts they employ and the relationship these concepts would have to other Christian churches on one hand, and ideologies on the other. The matter could not be settled by an *a priori* definition of religious belief. Such matters are left alone, first because of ignorance of the minutiae of peripheral Christian groups and secondly because they are peripheral. It should be stressed here that the religious and theological attitudes outlined are *examples* of Christian thought, not archetypes.

As for ideology, this is seen as including Marxism, liberalism and conservatism amongst others, though again no hard and fast lines can be drawn. What can, and cannot, be said to be ideological depends on the examination of individual cases and what connections can be drawn between the examples we have in mind. The fact that this may be difficult (consider the relationship between conservatism and anarchism or the women's movement) should not lead us, however, to suppose that there are no lines to be drawn. Indeed, one of the problems located in Patrick Corbett's analysis is that he seems unwilling to draw any lines at all between Catholicism, myths about English public schools or almost any kind of belief that is held by a number of people and influences their actions. The view of ideologies in Chapter 2 does, to a certain extent, presuppose some of the sceptical conclusions that are advanced in other parts of this book, especially that the ideologies named above have failed to establish themselves as 'objective' accounts of political activity to the exclusion of their rivals.

A further point here is that a view of religion and ideology (as characterised above) emerges in Chapter 2 in terms of elucidating certain characteristic arguments and activities. The place, then, to see what is meant by religion and ideology is at the end of the chapter, not in the search for a definition or definitions at the outset. Mr Rashid's point that seemingly obvious objections may have to be set aside till the end before we can see whether they are appropriate or not is pertinent here.

But what of the two possible views of the relationship between religion and ideology that are rejected? The first approach to be considered, holds, roughly speaking, that they are distinct. This view is often held by religious believers and ideologists who see themselves as potential rivals. The religious believer may assert for example, that religion is concerned with 'divine' properties, whereas ideology is a thoroughly secular enterprise. Though God does play an important part in religious life, this does not mean that religion has nothing to do with secular affairs – it merely judges them by different standards such as the canons of biblical revelation or whether they accord with the *Lex Divina*. Clerical politicians such as the Rev. Ian Paisley or those opposed to the 1967 Abortion Act are not exceeding the demands of their calling by indulging in political activity, they are claiming that the standards of the Bible *ought* to be the standards of secular political life. This is a legitimate, if somewhat hopeful, enterprise.

On the other hand, ideologists such as Marx have wished to express the difference they see between religious thought and their own analysis of the world in terms of the distinction between the rational and the irrational. Religious beliefs are seen as false-consciousness or wish-fulfillment. By his own standards, therefore, Marx was quite consistent in not attempting to refute religious beliefs, since, if the believer is in the grip of false-consciousness no *argument* will be of any avail. For Marx, what is needed is socialism, not scholasticism. This will, of course, strike religious believers as plainly unfair, as each utterance, not matter how reasonable it seems, just adds more grist to the Marxist mill. It is the same feeling that attends the victims of psychoanalysis. But the fact that nothing can count against Marx's characterisation discredits rather than confirms it as a thesis. The conclusion is that Marx and those who argue along similar lines have confused reasons as grounds with reasons as motives and have, therefore, not shown religious beliefs to be irrational at all. All such an argument could show would be that Marxism *and* religion are both products of certain material conditions and neither rational nor irrational. As Dr Graham points out, there is no need for a *special* explanation here.

The point alluded to in this first section, and brought out by the examples in the second part, is that religion and ideology can play the same role in a person's life. That is, as someone may see themselves as saved through the power of God's love, revealed in Jesus, so another may believe that 'exploitation' and 'alienation' will be at an end when the 'expropriators' are 'expropriated' by the 'proletarian revolution'. It is the undeniable force of such parallels that has led some philosophers to conclude that Marxism is a religion or Christianity an ideology. Whether or not this attitude is part of the legacy of logical positivism is not, strictly speaking, relevant here.

Corbett seems to hold that outside logic and science is a ragbag of topics (ethics, theology, and the like) that are the province of 'practical reason' and that there is no point in distinguishing between the forms that this kind of reasoning may take. The important distinction is between *logic* and practical reasoning. This will, of course, not do either as an account of the relationship, if any, between the reasons put forward in religious and those advanced in ideological arguments.

One suggestion is that human 'reason' has progressed from primitive religion to Christianity and then to ideologies, each stage being an advance on the former. This is one interpretation of Alasdair MacIntyre's position, namely, that Marxism has *replaced* Christianity in the secular world. The truth or otherwise of this assertion cannot be established just by finding out if Christianity pre-dates anything we consider to be ideological thought, any more than the decline of Christianity and rise of science in importance in our culture could establish that science has refuted religion. What is needed is a conceptual link, and this is what MacIntyre and Corbett hope to provide by suggesting that religion and ideology are answers to the *same* question. As has been admitted, the parallels are there, but it would appear that both MacIntyre and Corbett pay too much attention to what Wittgenstein called the 'surface grammar' and not enough to the 'depth grammar' of the subjects involved.

How does this distinction between surface and depth grammar show itself here? The first way is in the role of faith in religious thought. Ideologists often try to base the certainty of their prescriptions for political action on conclusions reached in science, history, or philosophy. Whatever the merits of this attempt (which are dealt with elsewhere), religion is not so based. Even though some religious philosophers have tried to establish valid proofs for the existence of God, theology and for that matter religion itself do not depend upon the success of such arguments. It is instructive to note that Aquinas claims that Christian teaching rests on that which is too high for human knowledge and revealed by God.[2] In short, theology is *subordinate* to faith, and the theologian does not question God's revelation any more than the scientist questions the uniformity of nature. Religion then is not based upon science or philosophy (and not theology either, since theology is another *facet* of religion).

118 The Form of Ideology

The second area in which distinctions can be drawn between religious and ideological thought is in the content of the respective beliefs. Central here is the concept of the *eternal* in religious thought. This must not be confused with *endless duration*. As is pointed out, a Marxist could see the defeat of the General Strike as an event which will be overcome at a later date but the Christian does not see Jesus's death as a defeat which turned out to be a victory; eternally understood, it always is a victory. This is connected with the part played by the after-life in religious thought. The issues are complex, but one point worth making is that while the post-revolutionary society of Marx and Engels will still be a historical one, the post-Resurrection one is not.

There is, then, for the Marxist, the possibility of abolishing alienation and exploitation within history. But for the Christian, sin is a condition of man's existence that can only be fought against, not removed.

The fact that religious *beliefs* make a difference to religious activities does not, as Peter Winch points out,[3] mean that they are theories upon which these activities are based; rather, the beliefs are implicit in the activities. This means that a ritual is not the same where 'X' is substituted for 'God' – the grammar is different – and that external similarities between activities are not as important as the *internal* connections between the ritual and the beliefs that go with it. Religious rituals express certain attitudes that are absent in ideological activities. A final point here is that the difference between ideologies and religion that has been suggested in terms of the form and content of the arguments employed by both is itself not a difference between people who hold opposing theories. Although both are 'trying to explain why the world is as it is', they are not offering rival accounts of the same set of phenomena in the way that two scientists might do. The fact that they are 'about everything' does not entail that they are another way of saying everything, or explaining everything. They may come into conflict with each other, but they are not rivals in the way that two scientific theories would be. The ideologist does not give an incorrect answer to the questions asked by the religious believer; for he does not ask a religious question but ignores religion as a way of looking at things. And, of course, vice versa.

Although Chapter 3, 'Ideology and Philosophy', is not only about the character and scope of MacIntyre's attempt to relate these two forms of understanding, as a book review might be, it is primarily so. It obviously must be read alongside at least those parts of MacIntyre's volume to which extensive reference is made. Of course this does not mean that there are not points of some generality which might be pursued further afield. Of these one in particular is important in the context of the philosophical investigation of the claim that ideological commitment can derive strength from philosophical inquiry. It concerns the illustration of a certain kind of difficulty in philosophical criticism where the critic, although he professes to be in search of understanding of his object, may get in his own way, as it were, in insisting too much and too soon that he finds the object unintelligible. The illustration given is that of the critic who immediately rejects the claim that squaring the circle is something we can attempt to do. Even where this critic may think something justifies him in claiming the unintelligibility of his object, it is argued that such thoughts may need to be hushed if he is to give himself a chance to comprehend what may only appear to be unintelligible.

According to the sketch given of the critic B's thinking, he took 'logic' to be on his side, against the circle-squarer. Nothing is said to endorse this view, which may be mistaken, but it is a view that is so manifestly plausible as to discourage serious consideration of the claim that squaring the circle can be attempted. Something of the same response is likely to be provoked by MacIntyre's claim that philosophy is not a single inquiry, indeed that some ideology is philosophy. People do, apparently, speak of particular philosophies: X's philosophy as distinct from Y's, a new philosophy and old ones, and so on. Our response is all too likely to be that where this does not mean one doctrine or system, rather than another, and so really does seem to be a denial that philosophy is a single inquiry, this mode of speech is obscure, when a lot more needs to be said as to why and in what way 'philosophy' does fail to constitute a single inquiry or discipline.

Nevertheless, it is still reasonable to think that MacIntyre would find difficulty in arguing alone such lines as: Christianity is one ideology, while Marxism and Freudianism are others; analogously, X is one philosophy, while Y and Z are others. It is difficult to know what would be possible candidates for these variable spaces. (It seems quite another matter to speak of various doctrines or traditions. There seems nothing wrong with speaking of Platonism, idealism, solipsism, constructivism, phenomenalism, and so on, as distinctive doctrines, that do not together form one large doctrine. Conversely, logic, metaphysics, ethics do form philosophy, but as subjects, not as doctrines.)

In so far as we do not know what talk of one particular philosophy rather than another would amount to in various cases, we do not have any reason at present to suppose that the view attributed to MacIntyre would necessarily be less vulnerable to the objections advanced just because such talk might (already) have some genuine application. It would have to be an application that went along with

120 The Form of Ideology

other things that MacIntyre and similarly inclined thinkers would want to say. As it stands MacIntyre has not shown us where the philosophical foundations of ideology are located and what they support that can be expressed in ideological terms.

The thesis of Chapter 4, 'Ideology and Theoretical Inquiry', consists of the proposal that in considering ideology we should pursue a different epistemological account from that which we would give of a theory–practice relation. To make this point clearer we can refer to some remarks made by Otto Neurath on metaphysics and theology:

> The metaphysician and the theologian believe, thereby misunderstanding themselves, that their statements say something, or that they denote a state of affairs. Analysis, however, shows that those statements say nothing but merely express a certain mood or spirit. To express such feelings for life can be a significant task. But the proper medium for doing so is art, for instance lyric poetry or music. It is dangerous to choose the linguistic garb of a theory instead: a theoretical content is simulated where none exists. If a metaphysician or theologian wants to retain the usual meaning of language, then he must himself realise, and bring out clearly that he is giving not description but expression, not theory or communication of knowledge, but poetry or myth.[4]

It is the conclusion of Chapter 4 that the idea of political theory cannot be sustained, but it should be made clear that it is not intended that ideology should be considered as merely the expression of a certain mood or spirit. In fact the author believes that the contrast between description and expression, that is, between theory or communication of knowledge and poetry and myth, is either too simple or question-begging to account for the nature of ideological understanding. In addition it is thought that the suggestion that a theoretical content is simulated where none exists can be positively misleading unless properly understood in its application to ideology.

It is argued in Chapter 4 that ideological understanding can be usefully considered as the presentation of an ideal or ideals as being realistic possibilities. It should be noted here that the term ideal does not in itself imply optimism; whether a man is optimistic or pessimistic is to be understood in terms of the ideals that he feels able to subscribe to. In short, then, ideology is seen as a response to Plato's question: *how should men live?*; a response which justifies a recommendation both by making it intelligible and by displaying its rationality, that is, by saying how it is that we have good reasons for seeing this as a realistic and not merely imaginary possibility. With these remarks in mind the author sought to indicate the place of a picture of man in ideological understanding. This metaphor stands in need of explication. (The term conception is not a good sustitute.) One account can be given which runs as follows. In it the notions of a response and of an answer to a question are distinguished, and it is argued that a picture of man is necessary to the intelligibility of any particular answer to the question of how men should live.

So far it has been suggested that an ideological response to this problem rendered intelligible a specific answer, or set of specific answers. For example, let us suppose that a particular answer consisted of the recommendation that we should not have the institution of, or, better, right to, private property. Now this is obviously a quite different recommendation from, say, saying that we should do without milk, although the question of whether we should be vegetarians is analogous. The absence of a right to private property would bring about a very large change in the relations of men, and it is not at all obvious that such a change can be readily comprehended. What we want is an account of the entailments involved in what is presented as a stark possibility – it is an account of the entailments, in terms of rationality, that the ideologist's response to the question of how we should live consists of (in the example cited we can contrast socialist and anarchist conceptions of property, and of life in the absence of it). In this sense the ideologist's picture or conception of man constitutes a hinterland of beliefs that serve to specify the sense of the substantive questions and answers that are offered by people attempting to give an answer to the very general question mentioned above.

The important question of the objectivity of what has been referred to as a hinterland of belief still remains and this is the form of the logical positivists' charge that 'a theoretical content is simulated where none exists'. Following on some suggestions made by Hilary Putnam in his essay 'Literature, science and reflection',[5] it may be possible to sustain the suggestion that the ideological understanding consists of *conceptual knowledge*, that is, the kind of knowledge necessary for the explication of possibilities associated with the relations that men can and should have with one another. Ideological thinking thereby engages the ethical imagination. It engages it in the abstract in a way analogous to its involvement in the work of the poet (taking poetry in the widest, and literal, sense to mean artistic activity as such). The objectivity of this use of language thereby resides just in the fact that *we* go on using it in the evaluation of our lives and practices, the fact that we do use it to speak of ourselves. It is not knowledge, because it is not testable, but it does not follow from this, if the idea of conceptual knowledge is coherent, that it is mere expression as Neurath would have us believe.

The Form of Ideology

In Chapters 4 and 5, 'Ideology and Theoretical Inquiry' and 'The Place of Ideology in Political Life', the argument is advanced that ideology does not take the form of a theory that can, in a technical sense, be put into practice in the conduct of political life. It may express an attitude to human relationships and activities that has political significance, but it cannot instruct us in the business of successfully changing those relationships and practices. Ideology does not provide us with information of the kind employed by the engineer and weather forecaster, because it is not theoretical in the way that the discipline of sicence is theoretical.

The discipline of science provides us with theoretical knowledge of a natural process. It permits the construction of coherent accounts of the logical relationships between verified hypotheses asserting causal relationships between measured phenomena. In other words, the explanatory power of a scientific theory, that is, that which makes it a theory, is dependent on the relationships it is claimed exist between a set of hypotheses being as consistent with one another as each of those hypotheses is experimentally verifiable. A theory said to be formulated within the discipline of science which does not possess this consistency is as much a confused formulation as a proposition about a causal relationship that cannot be confirmed is irrelevant to the theory's successful formulation. The conceptual framework of the confused formulation simply will not apply to the phenomena it is claimed it explains.

To conceive of ideology as generating theoretical knowledge about ideal human relationships derived from an investigation of human nature and history cannot be held to make sense when neither the required coherence nor the relevant empirical investigation is a possible achievement. In Chapters 4 and 5 the attempt is made to show that this is the case, that is, that ideological talk does not refer to the world. Conceived as theory, ideological talk is conceptually incoherent in that it is incapable of empirical verification. Acceptance of this conclusion, however, does not entail that we must affirm that ideological statements have neither sense nor force. It merely eliminates the possibility that we can consistently affirm that their sense and force is that of technical information supplied by theoretical formulae.

The critique of ideology as theory is not a Trojan horse in the ideologist's camp capable of demoralising and scattering its defenders. Its proper place in the study of ideology is more that of a peragogic device than of an engine of war. Ideological writing may consist of a *prima facie* confusion of theoretical with practical reasoning, or the investigatory with the evaluative mode of thought, but this need not destroy its relevance to political life, or refute the claim that it constitutes an essential constituent of political involvement. The rejection of the claim that ideology can assist us in the formation of informed intentions does not preclude our considering it as the medium in which the members of a group or party can express their commitment, as distinct from gain instruction in the management of their affairs. Moreover, the claim in Chapter 5 that ideological writing is incapable of generating a technical vocabulary, of the kind we find deployed in a court of law, does not imply that terms such as 'reform', 'revolution' and 'liberation' cannot be related to events in a way that has political significance. To call the Russian Revolution of 1917 a 'revolution' in the Leninist sense does not indicate that it is an example of the same kind of event as the Hungarian Revolution of 1956. Ideological terms do not specify which do, and which do not, belong to a class of events. Disputes between Leninists and Trotskyists over whether or not the Russian and Hungarian Revolutions are both 'revolutions' are disputes about the authentic Marxist use of the term 'revolution', not disputes about what happened in Russia in 1917 and Hungary in 1956. In a world of changing political situations the opportunities for innovation within an ideological tradition are such that the success of any attempt to determine, within a tradition, the authentic use of any one ideological term is likely to be short-lived. However, that ideological disputes are interminable does not imply that they are insignificant. There is something at stake although it is not a matter of historical fact. What is at stake is the assessment of the political significance of events by persons whose conclusion indicates a preference for a particular approach to political issues. The ideologist who claims that both the Russian and Hungarian Revolutions are 'revolutions' in the Marxist sense clearly subscribes to a different interpretation of Marxism than those who also claim to be Marxist and do not. So central is the term 'revolution' to the Marxist tradition of discourse that those who claim to be Marxists and differ as to its 'correct' application are unlikely to find common membership of any one group or party congenial. Although questions of ideological orthodoxy cannot determine what a particular group or party should do, they do have direct bearing on the motivation of its members. Members of a group or party who are dissatisfied with the outcome of any one ideological confrontation and, for reasons of party discipline, are obliged to suppress their opinion, may well decide to leave and form another group or party the policy of which may be distinct from that which they have previously seen fit to support.

The question now arises: what is it that makes a particular policy and style of execution appropriate to a particular example of ideological understanding? In so far as the ideology in which a group of adherents believe is taken to be a theory prescribing a particular course of action, adopting that course of action will appear to them to be the rational choice, but since the belief that an ideology is theoretical is mistaken, the policy it is taken to prescribe cannot be the rational choice. The relationship between the ideology and the policy can be no more than one of contingency. However, this does not imply that certain decisions cannot be seen to be appropriate for those who hold certain beliefs. The relationship between ideology and policy being contingent does not preclude a policy being preferred by a particular group of adherents and, when pursued over a period of time, readily identified as peculiar to their organisation. Indeed, it is difficult to avoid identifying particular policies with an ideology when they have been devised by those who claim to act in its name, and who justify its adoption in the vocabulary of the appropriate tradition of discourse. We do not have to show that an ideology can be put into practice to defend the view that it is the privilege of those who have formed a group or party in the name of an ideology to determine what actions are to be taken as an expression of belief in it. We can legitimately affirm that Leninism cannot be separated from the 'liquidation of the Kulaks' and national socialism from the decision to murder millions of Jews in the name of the 'final solution', in spite of the fact that Leninism does not demonstrate that the murder of millions of small landowners is a step towards bringing about 'communism', and national socialism does not demonstrate that putting millions of Jews in gas chambers is a step towards the spiritual regeneration of the 'Aryan race'.

Joining an ideologically oriented group or party is an act of commitment to a certain life-style. To express this commitment it is not enough to deploy the vocabulary of the relevant ideology when an evaluation of events and relationships is called for: participation in the activities of a formal organisation is required. An ideological vision of experience creates the possibility of a world of imagined events and relationships in which posters, banners, flags, uniforms, songs, displays, rallies and marches may all serve to express what admittedly does not exist in the world, but, in the minds of those who find them meaningful, should exist and will exist when their cause is triumphant. The activities of the ideologically committed are in many respects an elaborate ritual. Their performance is senseless for those who do not share the commitment and their performance by the uncommitted cannot express any commitment, but for those who are committed certain activities are meaningful because they have decided that they do express their beliefs. The serious members of Lenin's Bolshevik Party are not 'communists' and the serious members of Hitler's National Socialist Party are not *Herrenvolk* in the eyes of the sceptic, but this cannot prevent the committed conceiving that their rituals are a manifestation of the struggle to become what they believe they are destined to be.

It is not a sufficient explanation of the murder of the 'Kulaks' and 'Jews' to state the intentions of those who selected and implemented the two policies in terms of what it was they thought they could achieve in practice. For those morally responsible for the two policies of mass extermination these were not simply a matter of expediency, even if they were expedient in any material sense. Their executions were symbolic acts in the same way that the terrorist's action of killing a policeman can be symbolic. The policeman may be murdered, not because the terrorist intends to diminish the chances of his being arrested on a charge of belonging to an illegal organisation, but because he is seen by the terrorist to represent, for example, the 'capitalist state'. The policeman's murder can be represented in the vocabulary of the ideology of the terrorist as a case of the 'proletariat' destroying 'capitalism'. Similarly the murder of the 'Kulaks' can be represented as a case of 'class war' and the murder of the 'Jews' as an example of the 'struggle between races'. Understanding ideologically motivated actions requires an appreciation of the correct deployment of the appropriate ideological vocabulary. Given access to the relevant documents the students of history can determine who gave the orders to kill the 'Kulaks' and 'Jews' and the reasons for the conclusions that these policies were efficacious. Given access to the works of Lenin and Hitler, the student of ideologies can determine how we are to understand the appropriateness, for the ideologically committed follower, of Bolshevik and National Socialist Party policies through the correct deployment of the vocabulary of their ideologies.

The historian's task is one of investigating the documentary evidence for past events and actions with a view to forming the most plausible of possible accounts of what has happened in the world. The student of ideology's task is one of examining texts with a view to forming the most perspicuous representation of particular ideological visions. Both are essential to the study of politics. No less essential is the philosophical investigation of the relationship between ideology and action which determines the place of ideology in political life.

It will no doubt be said in criticism, both of Chapter 6, 'The Uses of Ideological Language', and of other chapters in this book that it is nowhere entirely clear what its authors understand by ideology. In a collection which addresses the question of the form of ideology, this charge, if true, would indeed be unfortunate. It might, for example, be argued that the author of Chapter 6 has merely advanced 'his account' of ideology, with no good reason for anyone else to follow it, even if the critic manages to reconstruct how the author uses the word in the first place. This criticism is, however, a misunderstanding, and derives from a mistaken account of how to proceed in investigating the concepts appropriate to understanding political practice.

The critic who makes the above point would presumably require an account of the use of ideological language to commence with a definition: a stipulation of how the term ideology is to be understood when readng the book. If this were done we might draw up a list of writers, or writings, which such a definition would include, and another list of those it would exclude. However, the defence of such a list could only be made on pragmatic grounds: that it is more or less useful, plausible, or appropriate in the understanding of political practice as opposed to some competing definitions. These definitions have been arrived at in many ways, for example, by examining how the term has been most influentially used in the past (Plamenatz),[6] or by attempting to include as many competing definitions as is humanly possible (Seliger).[7] However, all these approaches suffer from a crippling defect: they do not so much illuminate an aspect of political practice as *demand* that we understand it in this manner or that if we are to follow their argument, which is surely to put the cart before the horse. In general these authors are not so much puzzled by an aspect of the practice of politics as puzzled by the inability of fellow theorists to understand the practice in quite the same terms as they do. Thus such accounts very easily degenerate into confrontations between opposing schools of thought.

Instead of succumbing to this temptation, the aim of Chapter 6, and indeed of the book in general, has been to examine an aspect of political life which seems to have been poorly comprehended in the past. It should be made clear that the point of the introductory consideration and rejection of the arguments of de Tracy, Marx and Mannheim is not to suggest that in some sense they have mis-described an aspect of reality, which would imply that we are left with a clearly marked-out subject matter which just does not happen to fit their descriptions. There is obviously something very wrong with this formulation, but it stems directly from the manner in which the critic would have us proceed. Instead, it should be pointed out that we have argued that there is nothing which could meet his requirements. The argument against Marx, for example, is not to be understood to be claiming simply that ideology is not a class-bound (mis-)perception of some 'social reality', but that, since there can be no such perception, the term ideology in Marx's writing is either meaningless or is to be understood in some other sense altogether. So, when we come to consider writings which self-consciously refer to 'liberals' or 'socialists' we are merely concerned in the first instance to discover which concepts are appropriate to the ideas being expressed in such writings. This leaves entirely open the question of whether ideology is a useful term or not, that is, whether it refers to something distinctive in political life, or whether it should disappear along with the epistemological confusions of its progenitors. It seems to have escaped the critic's notice that if we were to proceed, as he wishes, by stipulative definition, such an option would not be open, except as a bald assertion.

Thus we see the point of the method utilised in Chapter 6. It is surely understood that it contains sufficient reference to the kind of literature under consideration, and a further review would merely be repetition. We proceed by considering the argument that so-called ideological writings are either moral or technical, and show that sufficient differences exist to reject such an attempt to subsume them under either of these headings. Similarly a distinction is drawn between the manner in which the argument is deployed, and the conceptual nature of the content, which suggests the essentially practical locus of such arguments. Having cleared away these misunderstandings, we are left with the problem of how such an apparently novel use of language conveys meaning, and the latter half of the chapter is taken up with various more or less well worked out suggestions, the most important having to do with the place of metaphor in political language. It is the implications of this latter suggestion which require further comment, lest some of the enthusiasm which has been expressed for it be resting on further misconceptions.

It was argued that the ideological use of language was essentially an imaginative one, and that the act of imagination involved making connections between the technical functions of political practices and particular dispositions amongst citizens. The nature of these dispositions was left unclear, as was the particular sense of 'imagination' upon which much of the argument rests. Ideology seems to be concerned with political life seen under the aspect of authenticity: something to be jealously preserved or earnestly striven for. Of course, rules, institutions and courses of action in the world have to be described in technical terms, but our attitude towards them, the attitude which we express in words and our actions, is of another order, and it is with this attitude that ideology is concerned.

Although great pains were taken to emphasise that not all political ideology could be understood as metaphorical, it is perhaps not so clear that, given the account in the chapter, all political metaphor is not ideological. Furthermore, if ideology is merely an exercise of the imagination connected with politics this does not appear to tell us very much of interest. After all, it may be argued, imagination is required to be a successful historian or even a technologist. This is to overlook the fact that the sense of imagination which interests us is not merely that of a psychological faculty, which we all possess to some degree, but to distinguish the creative use of language from that which is a contribution to a discipline. The point is not that the latter is bound by rules and the former is 'free', 'unguided', or whatever for no such distinction could be maintained if we are ever to understand an imaginative piece of work. It is that the relation of the imaginative work to the rules is different in important ways. These differences are explored in aesthetics, and it is here that we should look for the relationship between political ideology and political practice.

The connection with metaphor is a contingent one, as indicated in the text. It just happens to be a very efficient way of expressing our concern with authenticity in conduct, when characterising practices. But it is only political metaphors which actually express such concerns which are ideological – metaphors can perfectly happily appear in other contexts. I certainly do not mean to suggest that Hobbes's *Leviathan* is an ideological text. However, our concern with metaphor is obviously connected to our concern with imagination, for it provides the clearest counter-example to the objection that 'seeing-as' is an incoherent concept in the context of ideology. What a study of a particular metaphor could show is how the ideologist draws upon contemporary conceptions of social arrangements and the historically distinct vocabularies in which they are expressed. Intellectual historians who claim to perceive 'climates of opinion' are not completely misguided. Their search for the intellectual precursors of more successful writers, 'the roots of Nazism' or 'the intellectual background of liberalism', may have something to offer us if we understand it as providing evidence of what is referred to as 'the stock of ordinary words and phrases' which the ideologist may draw upon. That is, we are not to understand such investigations as explaining why liberalism or national socialism should appear at this or that time with such success, but as showing a language having an appropriateness in the manner in which it is deployed by particular ideologists at particular times. Our investigation is in fact to illustrate the plausibility of an account of meaning, not to explain the existence or non-existence of certain states of affairs; it is philosophical, not historical.

In particular, it requires to be shown exactly what could be conveyed by such a sentence as, for example, 'understand these actions as a symptom of mass society'. In order to produce an account of the meaning of such a statement which would develop the theme of Chapter 6, one line of argument must be shown to be valid. It must be possible to substantiate the claim that we can learn to use such phrases as 'mass society' independently of our being able to specify the particular actions and institutions which allegedly make it up. In other words 'mass society' must be shown to be more than just a redescription of something which could be perfectly adequately described in more straightforward language. Now in order to show that a liberal and a socialist mean something quite different by 'the masses', it must be possible to say that while they both perceive the poor they take different attitudes towards them and it is just this difference of attitude which is inseparable from the meaning of 'the masses' when it appears in an ideological context. It is what this attitude is an attitude of which specifies the context as ideological rather than ethical. We have referred to this as authenticity in politics because it seems to convey the difference between ideological concerns and the kind of absolute-value considerations which are the domain of ethics.

We find an excellent example of the confusion involved in taking ideology to be description, and its consequences, in Ernest Nolte's *Three Faces of Fascism*[8] where it is claimed that the success of *Action Française* can be explained by pointing to the fact that the Third Republic was the first example of 'mass democracy' in Europe, by which is presumably meant the first example of universal male franchise. However, the author cannot then go on to show how *Action Française* used the term 'the masses' in the sense of a crushing weight of mediocrity, without making it clear that this is not the same sense of mass as in 'mass democracy', or else he courts circularity. 'The masses' used ideologically is clearly not a descriptive term, as 'mass democracy' is meant to be (whether it is or not is another matter).

This is why Chapter 6 lays such stress on the fact that metaphors are not descriptions. (As it stands it is considerably watered down from the theses expressed here, for it merely suggests these directions without actually showing that a sound case can be made for them). A case *is* made for considering ideological writings to be imaginative uses of language, in the sense of 'seeing as', and the point is made that this rules out any kind of straightforward description. If we continue to have the model of description (let alone explanation) before our eyes, we shall always have a puzzle about ideology. It has become commonplace to hear that ideological statements are 'beyond verification'. This is often put forward by those who have vaguely heard somewhere that nasty logical positivism, which claimed that such statements are meaningless, has now been 'refuted', and they fondly imagine that they now have a category where recalcitrant uses of language can be shunted off without further explanation. Chapter 6 could be seen as an attempt to explore just what 'beyond verification' could mean in the case of ideology.

The authors of this book have undertaken an investigation of the form of ideology. It would be to have misread it to conclude that they have in any way attacked ideology. The work provides no reasons grasping which must diminish any rational man's adherence to any set of ideological beliefs. It undermines only those accounts of ideology the authors hold to stand in the way of an adequate understanding of the place of ideology in life. These accounts are presented as a barrier to our grasping what ideology is, because they deny that it has any autonomy as a display of intellect. They portray it as dependent on the findings of a recognised discipline, epiphenomenal or confused. It is said to be parasitic, unreflective, or irrational thinking about the world of human relationships. Whether it is presented as something we need, or would be better off without, ideology, in the rejected accounts, is characterised as a theoretical formulation said to offer technical guidance in the conduct of political affairs. It is this fundamental misconception of ideology which has obscured the fact that ideological convictions are something that we hold. They are not something that we demonstrate. We have ideological beliefs in a world, not ideogolical knowledge of the world, and, consequently, to portray ideology as theory is radically misleading. It directs us to undertake the hopeless task of trying to prove which ideology, or part of an ideology, is true and which false, when the form of ideology is not one in which truth tests have application. We declare an ideological conviction by elaborating its assertions and participating in activities deemed to express adherence to its principles. We do not demonstrate its claims by conducting an investigation. The medium of ideological communication is imagination, not analysis and proof. What the ideologically committed affirm is an aspiration in life. In short, the logic of arguments and the substantiation of accounts that fall within the province of academic disciplines do not fall within the ideologist's domain. They do not constitute the visions of human potential the ideologist believes to offer inspiration which themselves do not have to afford us knowledge.

There is a task which ideology can alone be seen to perform once it is regarded as an aspect of life, just as technology is an aspect of life – something without which the world we know could not be conceived. Attempts to dispose of ideology as the source of endless controversy and conflict involving enmity and war can only take the form of ideology. It is not an intellectual aberration. Man does not live by knowledge alone. Ideology is an autonomous display of intellect no less capable of masterly exposition than any other manifestation of man's creative powers. Philosophers would do well to give it serious consideration.

NOTES: POSTSCRIPT

1 L. Wittgenstein, *Philosophical Investigations* (Blackwell, Oxford, 1953), Preface, p. vii.
2 Thomas Aquinas, *Summa Theologiae*, Ia, 1 (Latin text and English tr. Blackfriars, London, 1964), p. 9.
3 P. Winch, 'Meaning and religious language', in *Reason and Religion*, ed. S. C. Brown (Cornell University Press, Ithaca and London, 1977), pp. 193–221.
4 O. Neurath, *Empiricism and Sociology*, ed. M. Neurath and R. S. Cohen (Reidel, Dordrecht, Holland/Boston USA, 1973), p. 307.
5 H. Putnam, *Meaning and the Moral Sciences* (Routledge & Kegan Paul, London, 1978).
6 J. Plamenatz, *Ideology* (Macmillan, London, 1971).
7 M. Seliger, *Ideology and Politics* (Allen & Unwin, London, 1976).
8 E. Nolte, *Three Faces of Fascism* (Weidenfeld & Nicholson, London, 1965).

Bibliography

Arnold, M., *Democratic Education*, ed. R. H. Super (Ann Arbor, Mich.: University of Michigan Press, 1962).
Black, M., *Models and Metaphors* (New York: Cornell University Press, 1962).
Burke, E., *Reflections on the Revolution in France* (Harmondsworth: Pelican, 1968).
Corbett, P., *Ideologies* (London: Hutchinson, 1965).
Drucker, H., *The Political Uses of Ideology* (London: Macmillan, 1974).
Flew, A. G. N., and MacIntyre, A. (eds), *New Essays in Philosophical Theology* (London: Macmillan, 1964).
Gallie, W. B., 'Essentially contested concepts', *Proceedings of the Aristotelian Society*, LVI, 1955-6, pp. 167-98.
Gardiner, P. (ed.), *The Philosophy of History* (London: Oxford University Press, 1974).
Harris, N., *Beliefs in Society* (Harmondsworth: Pelican, 1968).
Hegel, G. W. F., *Philosophy of Right* trans. T. M. Knox (London: Oxford University Press, 1967).
Hester, M. B., *The Meaning of Poetic Metaphor* (The Hague: Mouton, 1967).
Kierkegaard, S., *Purity of Heart*, trans. D. V. Steere (New York: Harper, 1956).
Lenin, V. I., *What Is To Be Done?*, trans. S. V. and P. Utechin (London: Oxford University Press, 1963).
MacIntyre, A., *Against the Self-Images of the Age* (London: Duckworth 1971).
Mannheim, K., *Ideology and Utopia* (London: Routledge & Kegan Paul, 1936).
Marx, K., and Engels, F., *The German Ideology* (London: Lawrence & Wishart, 1965).
Minogue, K. R., 'Epiphenomenalism in politics: the quest for political reality', *Political Studies*, vol. XX, no. 4, December 1972, pp. 462-74.
Murdoch, I., *The Sovereignty of Good* (London: Routledge & Kegan Paul, 1970).
Nolte, E., *Three Faces of Fascism* (London: Weidenfeld & Nicholson, 1965).
Oakeshott, M. J., *Rationalism in Politics* (London: Methuen, 1962).
Paine, T., *Rights of Man* (Harmondsworth: Pelican, 1969).
Phillips, D. Z., *The Concept of Prayer* (London: Routledge & Kegan Paul, 1965).
Phillips, D. Z., *Death and Immortality* (London: Macmillan, 1970).

Bibliography 133

Plamenatz, J., *Ideology* (London: Macmillan, 1971).
Pocock, J. G. A., *Politics, Language and Time* (London: Methuen, 1972).
Popper, K. R., *The Poverty of Historicism* (London: Routledge & Kegan Paul, 1957).
Putnam, H., *Meaning and the Moral Sciences* (London: Routledge & Kegan Paul, 1978).
Raphael, D., *Problems of Political Philosophy* (London: Macmillan 1970).
Rhees, R., *Without Answers* (London: Routledge & Kegan Paul, 1969).
Robinson, J. A. T., *Honest to God* (London: Westminster Press, 1963).
Runciman, W. G., 'False consciousness', *Philosophy*, vol. XLIV, no. 170, October 1969, pp. 303–13.
Seliger, M., *Ideology and Politics* (London: Allen & Unwin, 1976).
Smith, A., *Lectures on Rhetoric and Belles Lettres* (London: Nelson, 1963).
Spencer, H., *The Man Versus the State* (Harmondsworth: Pelican, 1969).
Strawson, P. F., *Freedom and Resentment and other Essays* (London: Methuen, 1974).
Tawney, R. M., *The Radical Tradition* (Harmondsworth: Pelican, 1966).
Tucker, R., *The Marxian Revolutionary Idea* (London: Allen & Unwin, 1970).
Wilson, B. (ed.), *Rationality* (Oxford: Blackwell, 1970).
Winch, P., *Ethics and Action* (London: Routledge & Kegan Paul, 1972).
Wittgenstein, L., *Tractatus Logico-Philosophicus* (London: Routledge & Kegan Paul, 1961).
Wittgenstein, L., *Philosophical Investigations* (Oxford: Blackwell, 1953).
Wittgenstein, L., *Zettel* (Oxford: Blackwell, 1967).
Wittgenstein, L., 'A lecture on ethics', *The Philosophical Review*, vol. LXXIV, 1965.
Wittgenstein, L., 'Remarks on Frazer's *Golden Bough*', *The Human World*, May 1971.

Index

Academic disciplines 26, 66
Adherence 68, 80, 82, 86, 130
Alienation 31, 55, 64,
Amorality 81
Anabaptists 31
Anselm, St 29, 30
Aquinas, St Thomas 29, 30, 117
Aristotle 94
Arnold 90, 91, 93; *Democratic Education* 90
Atheism 25
Augustine, St 29
Austin, J. 53

Barker, F. 23
Barth, K. 26, 32
Belief 67, 68
Bentham, J. 104
Bible, The 31
Black, M., *Models and Metaphors* 105
Bourgeois revolution 32
Bultmann, R. 32
Burke, E. 92, 104, 107; *Reflections on the Revolution in France* 107, 108

Carlyle, T. 104
Catholic Church 2
Catholicism 27, 35
Causation 8, 9, 10, 57
Chesterton, G. K. 29
Christianity 22–4, 30, 34–5, 42, 48, 80
Civil Society 79
Class Struggle 31
Communist Society 79
Conceptual: difference 65; Knowledge 66; question 63; understanding 71
Corbett, P. 27, 28, 32, 115, 117; *Ideologies* 22, 27
Coup d'etat 75, 76
Crucifixion 34

Dialectical Laws 46
Dialectical Materialism 3, 7, 71

Disraeli, B., *Coningsby* 111
Divine Providence 45
Drucker, H. 28

Empirical investigation 44, 45
Engels, F. 44, 79
Epiphenomenalism 60, 61
Epistemological: incoherence 78; Justification 64
Eternity 33–5
Ethics 68, 69
Evolution 59

Faith 27, 30
False consciousness 24, 26, 31, 76, 116
Fascism 22
Feuerbach, L. 24, 25
Flew, A. G. N. 32; (with MacIntyre, A.) *New Essays in Philosophical Theology* 33
Forecasts 77
Frazer, J. 29
French Revolution 2
Freud, S. 24, 25

Gallie, W. B. 99, 103; 'Essentially Contested Concepts' 99
Gellner, E. 13; 'Concepts and Society' 13
General Strike 34
German Idealism 35
Giddens, A., *New Rules of Sociological Method* 98
Green, T. H. 79

Harris, N. 12, 13; *Beliefs in Society* 13
Hart, H. L. A. 53
Hayek, F. A. 102, 110
Hegel, G. W. F. 25, 55, 94, 98; *Philosophy of Right* 94
Hempel, C. G. 58
Hester, M. B. 106
Historical: contingency 76; investigation 91, 93, 96
History 32, 33

Index 135

History of political thought 91
Hitler, A. 73, 86, 99, 124, 125
Hobbes, T. 22, 128
Human Nature 55, 57, 59, 62–4
Hungarian Revolution 123

Ideological: argument 93, 95, 98–100, 103–4, 108, 110–11; commitment 40, 41, 78, 80–2, 87–8, 124; disputes 83–4; education 73, 87; imagination 100, 103; terms 76–8, 86, 103; tradition 100
Ideologies 2
Ideology: classical account of, 1, 3–4, 6–7, 10–11; Sociological notion of, 12–17, 19, 21
Imperialism 85

Job 24
John, St 23, 24
Judaeo–Christian tradition 23
Justifiable homicide 75, 76

Kant, I. 17
Kelsen, H. 53
Kierkegaard, S. 23, 26; *Purity of Heart* 3
Kingdom of God 32, 33

Language systems 91
Laws of nature 62
Legal identity 62, 63
Legal obligation 81
Lenin, V. I. 73–4, 78–9, 85–7, 109, 124–5
Liberalism 22, 84, 85, 114
Linguistic paradigms 91–2
Locke, J. 62
Logical Positivism 22
Luther, M. 60

MacIntyre, A. 27–31, 38, 40–52, 117–20; *Against the Self-Images of the Age* 28, 38, 41–4, 47–50
Maine, H. 104
Mandelbaum, M. 58
Mannheim, K. 4–8, 11–12, 54; Ideology and Utopia 5–6, 12
Marx, K. 2–8, 11–12, 24–6, 44, 54–5, 61, 64, 71–2, 74, 79, 86, 92, 98–9, 116, 126; *The Communist Manifesto* 63; *The German Ideology* 2; *Gesamtansgabe* 3
Marxism 22–4, 28, 30–2, 34, 42, 48, 55, 74, 78, 84–6, 99, 114, 123

Matthew St 23
Metaphor 104–8, 110, 127–8
Metaphysics 47
Meteorology 73, 77
Methodological objection 62
Mill, J. S. 29, 39, 71, 72, 79, 84
Minogue, K. R. 61; 'Epiphenomenaism in Politics: the quest for political reality' 61, 66
Moore, B. 102; *Social Origins of Dictatorship and Democracy* 102
Moral: argument 94, 95; duty 81; philosohpy 68
Morality 43
Murder 75–6
Murdoch, I. *The Sovereignty of Good* 51

Nationalism 22–3
National self-determination 31
Neurath, O. 121; *Empiricism and Sociology* 120
New Testament 24
Nolte, E. 129

Oakeshott, M. 71, 72, 74, 87, 88, 99, 103; *Rationalism in Politics* 73, 102
Old Testament 23, 24

Paine, T. 104, 108; *Rights of Man* 107–8
Party political relationships 73, 78, 82, 83, 87, 88
Paul, St 23, 24
Phillips, D. Z. 29, 33; *Death and Immortality* 34
Philosophical: criticism 40; inquiry 41, 45, 49, 50, 54; investigation 91, 113, 119, 125; Knowledge 42; results 50, 51; understanding 63
Philosophy of religion 30
Plamenatz J. 53, 54, 126
Plato 120
Pocock, J. G. A. 91, 92, 93; *Politics, Language and Time* 91
Political: activity 57, 72; conduct 71; education 72; identity 78; philosophy 66, 67; principles 71–3; rhetoric 93; theory 54, 56, 58–65, 67, 69
Polybius 92
Popper, K. R. 72–4, 87, 88, 98, 99, 103, 104

136 The Form of Ideology

Practical understanding 71
Prayer 24, 35
Prescriptive theory 67
Proletarian revolution 24, 31–3
Propositional context 62–4
Protestant sects 35
Psycho-analysis 28, 42
Putnam, H. 121

Raphael, D., *Problems of Political Philosophy* 22
Rationalisation 25
Rationalism 73, 75
Rationality 8–10, 18–19
Reductionism 25, 61
Reform 79
Religious: authority 31; community 24; tradition 30
Resurrection 24, 32, 33
Revolution 75–6, 79, 92, 99
Rhees, R., *Without Answers* 65
Robespierre, M. 73
Robinson, J. 30
Rule of law 32
Rules of conduct 79, 82
Russian Revolution 76, 78, 123

Salvation 31–3, 62, 80
Schleinermacher, F. D. E. 24
Science 31, 56–9, 62, 92, 113
Scientific: investigation 71; theory 122
Seliger, M. 126
Semantic intention 64
Smith, A. *Lectures on Rhetoric and Belles Lettres* 106
Socialism 43, 109
Sociological: investigation 12; understanding 12, 14

Sociology of knowledge 6, 11
Soviet Communist Party 74–5, 78
Spencer, H. 59, 79
Squaring the circle 39, 40, 66
Stalin, J. 75
Standards of conduct 79, 82
Stephen, F. T. 104
Stipulative definition 66, 114, 126, 127
Strauson, P. F. 104, 106; 'Categories' 104, 106–7

Tawney, R. H. 95, 96, 97; *The Radical Tradition* 95
Technical: argument 93–5; knowledge 77, 87; terms 75, 76
Technology 56, 58, 62
Theocratic government 33
Theology 29, 30
Theoretical knowledge 55, 62–3, 86, 122
Theory-practice relationship 56, 57, 62–3, 65, 67, 69, 71, 73–4, 83, 120
de Tracy, D. 2, 6–8, 11
Tradition of discourse 93, 98, 103

Utilitarianism 71
Utopia 100

Weltanschauungen 41, 50
Whitehead, A. N. 23
Winch, P. 118
Wittgenstein, L. 29, 65, 98, 105, 117; 'Notes on talks with Wittgenstein' 68; *Philosophical Investigations* 113; *Tractatus Logico-Philosophicus* 33–4; *Zettel* 101

For Product Safety Concerns and Information please contact our EU representative GPSR@taylorandfrancis.com
Taylor & Francis Verlag GmbH, Kaufingerstraße 24, 80331 München, Germany

www.ingramcontent.com/pod-product-compliance
Lightning Source LLC
Chambersburg PA
CBHW052130300426
44116CB00010B/1845